WHO really has the ANSWER?

Formerly *Who Is Worth Following*

WHO really has the ANSWER?

Formerly *Who Is Worth Following*

SPIROS ZODHIATES, Th.D.

AMG PUBLISHERS • CHATTANOOGA, TN 37421

First Printing 1976
Second Printing 1982
Third Printing 1989

ISBN 0-89957-514-5

Cover Design and Sketches: Florence Anderson

Printed in the United States of America

Dedication

Dedicated to my co-worker of many years,
Col. Constantine Kalonaros,
commemorating 25 years of our fellowship
together in the Lord's work
in the ministry of
AMG INTERNATIONAL
formerly
AMERICAN MISSION TO GREEKS

Preface

Are you perplexed as to a leader you can follow—and why you should follow him? Consider Jesus Christ. He gave two unique commandments at the beginning of His ministry that show His caliber. The first was a demand for a radical change in the life of His followers. That in itself is a demonstration of how extraordinary He is. No human leader would try to attract followers by telling them they needed to be changed. His chief concern would be to have as many followers as possible in order to enhance His popularity. But Christ was no mere human leader; He was God incarnate. He says to all who would follow Him, "Repent"—that is, be changed; that's the first thing you must do, before you can enter into fellowship with Him.

There are, of course, several commandments consequent to repentance, such as faith and baptism. What is the relationship between repentance, faith and baptism? Can one of these stand for the others? Is baptism, for instance, valid without repentance and faith? Is faith sufficient to get anyone to heaven? Is repentance possible without faith? When baptism is spoken of as saving us, does it include as its prerequisite repentance and faith? What is the relationship between repentance and forgiveness of sins? Can a person who has repented and exercised faith go to heaven without being baptized? Can anyone have repentance without faith or faith without repentance?

After His first commandment, Christ gave a second one: "Follow me." What does this involve? When you follow Christ, do you cease to be a realist as far as your environment is concerned and your own personal and social relationships? Is it wrong to make a living or own material possessions while you're following Christ? What sacrifices are necessary in order to follow Him? This book seeks to provide the Biblical answer to all these questions, and by the grace of God I endeavor to help you become a better follower of Jesus Christ.

Spiros Zodhiates
Ridgefield, New Jersey

Contents

DOES CHRIST COMMAND US TO JOIN ANY PARTICULAR CHURCH?

Just how is a Christian supposed to know what he may and may not do while on this earth? This question puzzles a great many honest, well-meaning Christians the world over. They are a bit vague as to whether Christ gave any specific commandments for them to follow. Did His teachings apply only to His times or are they eternal? Is Christ merely a historical figure, or is He contemporary? Do we need to go anywhere else other than the New Testament to find out how we should live a Christian life, how we should confront the world, the state, the various economic and political systems that have made their debut in our generation, and finally how we should make the everyday decisions that confront every one of us?

Because of this concern among Christians, we have been stimulated to examine the New Testament in the original Greek text to find out just what commandments Christ gave and to present these to you. We hope and trust that our lives will be deeply affected for good as we study together the requirements that the Lord Jesus laid down for every one of us.

As God looks down upon man, He recognizes only two classes of people in our world today—believers and unbelievers. Unfortunately, we have made many untrue, artificial, and humanly convenient divisions even within Christendom. We call ourselves Roman Catholics, Greek or Eastern Orthodox, Protestant, and the like. But God actually makes no such distinctions in His recognition of people. He cares very little whether you and I are Catholic, Greek Orthodox, Protestant, or anything else. These are all man-made divisions, an outcome of the activities of human beings, made for the convenience sometimes of themselves, sometimes of others, and sometimes of the society in which we live.

It is not that we are opposed to any denomination or religion. These are necessary as a matter of convenience in our religious affairs, even as are nations, communities, and families in our everyday world. Would the world be a better place if there were no nations or boundaries? Some theorists think it would, and that we would be far happier under such an arrangement. But who is to assure us that it would actually work out that way? There are some who are striving for a super-church today, a world church in which religious distinctions and denominations would be abolished. But we have serious doubts whether the church would get along any better and whether religion would be enhanced. Human organizational divisions are necessary conveniences, but they are not binding upon God. God recognizes only two classes: those who are actively related to Him, who have been reconciled to Him and thus are His children; and those who are not, who continue in the sin which they inherited from Adam as well as their own personal sin.

In the interests of truth, therefore, and in spite of our own organizational differences and conveniences, we must not be afraid to look at what God considers essential within the various religious groups.

A pious person who was perplexed by denominational differences had a dream. He thought that he had died and arrived at the gates of heaven. When he applied to the watchmen to admit him within the sacred walls, they inquired, "Whom do you want?" He replied that he belonged to the Independents and wished to join them in that place. "There are no such people here!" was the answer he received. "Well," said he, "I have had some connection with the Baptists; may I join them?" "We don't know any by that name," replied the heavenly watchmen. It was in vain that he asked for Episcopalians; they had never heard of them. There were not even any Wesleyans, or Catholics, or Greek Orthodox, or Presbyterians there. He was just going away in despair when, as a last resort, he said, "But I am a Christian." At this term the gates of bliss flew open, and he was received as a welcome guest. Being a Christian is the only thing that really matters in the sight of God. We may call ourselves by any other name, but, when we come to God, what counts is whether or not we are truly born-again Christians.

Many people today treat religion as a matter of convenience. They have to belong somewhere to be considered respectable. A clergyman once met an old schoolmate of whose activities he had long been ignorant, and finding him a judge of good standing congratulated him upon his success in life. As they were parting, the clergyman said to him, "And best of all, Judge, I find you are a member of our church." "Well," said the judge, "that's more a matter of chance than anything else. You see, when I was getting established in my profession, my wife and I thought we ought to join some church; it was more respectable. So, after mature deliberation, we settled down with a certain denomination and got on very well for a time; but they kept harping on 'faith, faith,' till we pretty soon discovered that they required more 'faith' than we had; so it became necessary to make a change. We turned the matter over considerably and at last, for various reasons, made up our minds to join another denomination. Here we found the demand was 'work, work' incessantly; and it was presently apparent that they demanded more 'work' than we were able to perform. It was with great reluctance that we concluded that we must change again, and we cast about with much caution, that this move might be final. At last we decided to connect ourselves with your church, sir, and have gotten along famously ever since without either faith or works."

Is this the kind of church member you are? Is this the kind of church that you have conveniently found? If so, you need to take a hard look at the teachings of the Lord Jesus Christ in order to determine whether you are really a Christian at all. He alone has given us the full revelation of God, for He was and is God come down to this earth to speak to us in our own human language, to tell what faith and works are required for us to please God and be once more connected with our creator in real blessedness and happiness. All of us are here in quest of happiness for our earthly lives. But when this life is ended, our eternal destiny will depend on what we have believed and done down here.

In the commandments of Christ, we shall find very explicitly what He expects us to believe and to do. Why go to anyone else, since we have the very words of Christ Himself? And in order to be absolutely sure that we understand what Christ said, what He commanded, let us examine the record in the original Greek language in which it was given to us by the inspired historians, Matthew, Mark, Luke, and John. Their testimony and records have stood firm through the centuries.

CHRIST'S ONLY COMMANDMENT TO THE UNCONVERTED

When a man is under a deep sense of guilt he finds great relief in unburdening himself. For this some will turn to their spiritual leader, another man, confessing their sins to him and looking to him for instruction as to how to live an upright and moral life. This is fine as long as this person knows Christ Himself and points men to the actual teachings of Christ. How shall we know whether he does or not? So many people are ignorant of what Christ actually commanded.

The safest course is for us to find out for ourselves by studying the Scriptures, so that we may be able to check whether we are being led aright or astray. This is most important, for it concerns not only our happiness here on earth but also our eternal destiny.

One commandment that we may be sure the Lord Jesus Christ never gave us is to go to our fellow men and accept their decrees for our lives. He said, "Now ye are clean through the word which I have spoken unto you. Abide in me, and I in you" (John 15:3, 4). The Word of Christ is the basic essential. Trustworthy spiritual leaders can and should bring it to us in as simple form as possible, but we shall do well to study it for ourselves. A good criterion as to whether our spiritual leaders are really giving us the Word of Christ is whether they encourage us to read it for ourselves.

A Brahmin said to a missionary: "We are finding you out. You are not as good as your Book. If you were as good as your Book, you could conquer India for Christ in five years." Sometimes it does not pay some people to have those whom they lead search the Scriptures themselves. But this is the only safe rule for those who would know the truth. It is in this task that we shall engage with respect to the commandments of Christ.

There is no doubt that the Lord Jesus Christ considered His words as commandments to be obeyed by all men. "He that hath my commandments, and keepeth them, he it is that loveth me" (John 14:21). And again, "If ye keep my commandments, ye shall abide in my love; even as I have kept my Father's commandments, and abide in his love" (John 15:10). Many who pretend to love Christ do not really keep His commandments. "If ye love me," He says, "keep my commandments" (John 14:15). But in order for us to keep His commandments we must first know them. And how many of us can enumerate the commandments of Christ? We would probably find it far easier to enumerate the Ten Commandments which God gave to Moses. It is not that these are not important; they are, which is why they are referred to so often by the Lord Jesus in His teachings. But the commandments of Christ are even more important, for they embody all that the commandments of God in the Old Testament set out to accomplish. Unfortunately, the commandments of the Old Testament were impossible to keep; while by contrast the commandments of the New Testament are possible because they are the fulfillment of the Old in Christ, who indwells the Christian. It is the indwelling Christ who enables us to worship the true God in spirit and in truth. It is Christ who enables us to see the truth about all the other false gods. It is He who can so transform us that His life within us becomes the fulfillment of the law. It is actually Christ within the believer who keeps the commandments in their totality and absoluteness. We are said to keep the commandments of Christ only as we die and He lives within us.

What was the first universal commandment

Christ gave to man? Chronologically first, that is. There is actually only one commandment which Christ gave to the whole world and the rest of the commandments are consequent to it. Only one commandment is given to unbelievers and all the others are given to believers. This is why the New Testament is primarily not a book for unbelievers but for believers. It speaks vividly of the world and the end to which it will come, but it speaks primarily to those who know God through Jesus Christ. That is why to those who do not know Christ, it hardly makes sense at times. For the child of God, however, it is food for the soul.

The birth of a child into the world, although basic and essential to life, is a very small part of his biography. He could have no biography without it. That is why most of the teaching of Christ concerns the growth of the believer, how he should live and behave. Many people, however, stress that part without first telling people how they can have life in Christ, how they can be born into the Kingdom of God. Thus the basic commandment of the Lord Jesus Christ, although short, is very much to the point. It is "Repent." We read in Matthew 4:17, "From that time Jesus began to preach, and to say, Repent: for the kingdom of heaven is at hand." This was the first message which the Lord Jesus Christ brought to the world. This is the first commandment addressed to all who have not made Jesus Christ their very own Lord and Redeemer.

This was not only Christ's first commandment but the first given by the Apostles. In Mark 6:12 we read, "And they went out, and preached that men should repent."

Before the Lord Jesus Christ ascended into heaven, He commissioned His followers to preach this message to the world. In Luke 24:47 we read, "And that repentance and remission of sins should be preached in his name among all nations, beginning at Jerusalem." This is the missionary message of the Church of Jesus Christ to all men.

When Peter stood before a great multitude on the Day of Pentecost, he was faithful to the commission of his Master, now departed, and said, "Repent, and be baptized every one of you in the name of Jesus Christ for the remission of sins, and ye shall receive the gift of the Holy Ghost" (Acts 2:38).

And when Paul stood on Mars Hill and preached to the heathen Greek philosophers, he had one basic message, the message of repentance. "And the times of this ignorance God winked at; but now commandeth all men every where to repent" (Acts 17:30).

The whole purpose of the coming of the Lord Jesus Christ to this earth is summarized in what He said in Matthew 9:13, "For I am not come to call the righteous, but sinners to repentance."

"Repent," then, is the basic commandment of the Lord Jesus and His preachers to the unconverted world. But what does repentance mean? When we hear Christ say "Repent," just what are we supposed to do? We shall consider this in our next study.

DOES REPENTANCE REQUIRE THOUGHT?

The only commandment which the Lord Jesus Christ gave to the entire world, that is to every individual, is to repent. This commandment is found in Matthew 4:17, "Repent: for the kingdom of heaven is at hand." Mark quotes Christ more fully when giving us His first commandment: "The time is fulfilled, and the kingdom of God is at hand: repent ye, and believe the gospel" (Mark 1:15). Luke and John made no particular reference to this first commandment.

In both Matthew and Mark, the word that is used for "repent" in the original Greek text is *metanoeite.* Irrespective of what we understand the English word to mean, we shall come nearer to our Lord's meaning by examining the original Greek word.

When we see a person doing wrong, we usually try to get him to change his conduct. But the Lord Jesus Christ did not go about it in this way. He was more interested in a change of mind, of heart, of the inner disposition of life. We do as we think; we act in accordance with what we are. Nobody can deny this fundamental truth. And yet when we seek a remedy for evil doing, we put the cart before the horse. In order that we may cease to *do* evil, we must cease to *be* evil. We cannot act differently unless we think differently. And we cannot think differently unless our inner beings, the dispositions of our thoughts and hearts, are changed. This inner change the Lord Jesus called *metanoia,* "repentance." "For as he [man] thinketh in his heart, so is he" (Prov. 23:7).

A Hindu said to a native missionary, "I am sure that if I lead a good life and do what is right, giving up my bad habits, God will be pleased with me and receive me into heaven." That is the way most people reason today. Replied the missionary, "You know the Babool tree (a tree with long, sharp thorns). Now, suppose you break off from its branches a hundred or more of the nasty thorns, will the tree on that account cease to be a Babool tree? Certainly not. Suppose you should apparently succeed in breaking off one or another, or even many, of your evil ways and habits, you would yet remain an evil tree, that is, a naturally bad man. You must have an entirely new nature, must become a new man, in order to please God; and only Christ can give you a new heart." The missionary's reply was sound and Scriptural. The message of Christ, His first and only message to sinful man, is his need of repentance.

Very interestingly, the Lord Jesus did not say that man should repent of one or another of his sins and evil habits, but just simply and plainly "repent." He does not preach to the thief to stop stealing, because he cannot do it. He does not preach to the adulterer to stop committing this particular sin, because he cannot. The Lord Jesus realizes one fundamental fact of life, that to eradicate symptoms one must erase the cause. The *sins* of man are the externalization of the *sin* of man. Christ did not come to make us quit our sins, but to enable us to acquire a new disposition, a new nature that is not inclined to sin but rather runs away from sin.

The verb *metanoeoo,* "to repent," is made up of the preposition *meta,* which means "after," and the verb *noeoo,* meaning "to perceive, to understand." In other words, to repent is to have an afterthought. *Metanoeoo* is the opposite of *pronoeoo,* which means to have a forethought. The one is afterknowledge and the other is foreknowledge. What Christ, then, commands is that every man have an afterthought about life, his own life.

Many people think that in order to come to

Christ we must cease to exercise our mental powers. Faith is taken to be the irreconcilable opposite of reason. But this is not Scriptural teaching. The first thing that the Lord Jesus Christ (who is called *ho Logos*, "the Word," meaning primarily "intelligence, logic") asks us to do is to think, to perceive, to know, to reason. He asks us to use that which He has given us. This commandment is addressed to man because only man has the capacity to think logically and to realize that he is not the product of mere chance; that there must be an intelligent Creator who has not divorced Himself from the world which He has created. The animals cannot arrive at that conclusion. The ability to think leads man to conclude that there is Someone above him who is beyond him and who made him.

To think is to grow in awareness. Stand before a flower and think. Stand before a sunset and think. Stand before the starry sky at night and think. Someone has said that the undevout astronomer is mad. "What do you see?" a friend asked a famous botanist who was scrutinizing a flower. "I see God," was the reverent answer. A Scottish doctor wrote with his finger in the garden soil the letters of his little son's name, sowed cress in the furrows, and smoothed the ground. Ten days after, his son ran to him in astonishment and said that his name was growing in the garden and insisted on his father seeing it. "Is it not a mere chance?" asked the father. "No, someone must have arranged it that way." "Look at yourself," said the doctor. "Consider your hands, fingers, legs, feet; did you come here by chance?" "No, something must have made me." "And who is that something?" As he did not know, the father told him the name of the great Being who had made him and all the world; and he never forgot that lesson. Think, man. Stand before a mirror and think. You are different from any one of billions of people who have lived on this earth, and yet in one sense you are the same. Stand before a corpse in a funeral parlor and think. Be observant. Think. Don't be afraid to think.

One of our most renowned scientists in this space age, Dr. Wernher von Braun, declared: "Today, more than ever before, our survival—yours and mine and our children's—depends on our adherence to ethical principles. Ethics alone will decide whether atomic energy will be an earthly blessing or the source of mankind's utter destruction. Where does the desire for ethical action come from? What makes us want to be ethical? I believe there are two forces which move us. One is belief in a last judgment, when every one of us has to account for what we did with God's great gift of life on earth. The other is belief in an immortal soul, a soul which will cherish the award or suffer the penalty decreed in a final judgment. . . . Belief in God," continues von Braun, "and in immortality thus gives us the moral strength and the ethical guidance we need for virtually every action in our daily lives. In our modern world many people seem to feel that science has somehow made such 'religious ideas' untimely or old-fashioned. But I think science has a real surprise for the skeptics. Science, for instance, tells us that nothing in nature, not even the tiniest particle, can disappear without a trace. Think about that for a moment. Once you do, your thoughts about life will never be the same. Science has found that nothing can disappear without a trace. Nature does not know extinction. All it knows is transformation! Now, if God applies this fundamental principle to the most minute and insignificant parts of His universe, doesn't it make sense to assume that He applies it also to the masterpiece of His creation —the human soul? I think it does. And everything science has taught me—and continues to teach me—strengthens my belief in the continuity of our spiritual existence after death. Nothing disappears without a trace." So concludes this great scientist as quoted in *This Week* magazine.

God has given us a mind with which to think, and if we think and think aright we cannot but arrive at the same conclusion as Dr. von Braun. We shall recognize that there is a part of man which cannot be weighed or seen and yet is just as real as that which can be detected by the physical senses. Look at a dead man. One moment he was active and alive, and the next he is incapable of moving his body. And yet the weight of his body immediately after death is exactly the same as it was a few minutes before. Only a fool would say that nothing had happened between life and death. Something that gave life to the body left him. What was it? Think. Serious thinking will lead us to know that we know very little and that there is something beyond our knowledge—the most important thing in life—that can come to us only by revelation: the personality of God.

The first step to repentance is directing our thoughts toward God our Creator. This is what Christ came to tell you and me. Will you think? It is only the fool who does not think, and he alone says that there is no God (Psalm 14:1). If you are not a fool, you must believe there is a God. But is this enough? We shall see.

LOOK BACK—THEN RUN TO CHRIST

Men believe many things without first thinking them through. But beliefs that will stand the test of time, that we can depend on and that we can successfully defend, are those which we have thought through and tested for ourselves. Rational belief is impossible without thinking, but thinking is not enough to enable a man to believe and be saved. Part of believing is thinking, but part of thinking is not necessarily believing.

The first, and actually the only commandment that the Lord Jesus Christ gave to all the people of earth was to repent. We have seen that this word in Greek, *metanoeoo,* literally means "to think afterward"; and that the primary step to repentance is for man to think—about himself, his origin, his destination—to *think,* period. But this thinking only leads us to the conclusion that we did not make ourselves, that there must be a God who is the ultimate Creator. Our thinking can go no further than that; it cannot lead to a personal understanding of God and a personal appropriation of Him. If God in His fullness could be known by thought, He would not have had to reveal Himself to man in a unique way, first through His prophets and then through His Son, the Lord Jesus Christ.

But why does Christ place primary stress, in His commandment to repent, not on mere thought but on afterthought? It's because man rejected forethought in Adam. When God created us, He told us to exercise forethought—to avoid sin by avoiding disobedience to Him. But we deliberately disobeyed God in our desire to elevate ourselves in knowledge and power beyond the limits prescribed by Him, choosing rather to believe Satan's lie. God meant man to take forethought (*pronoia*) of the consequences of sin. But having failed to do that, man now needs to exercise *metanoia,* "afterthought." Forethought, the weighing of sin and its consequences, can be exercised when man is in a state of reconciliation and communion with God, his Creator. *Metanoia* is the thought that comes after sin and the consciousness of sin. Man in his fallen state cannot avoid sin, cannot foresee sin; but he is called upon to "after-see," to recollect and reflect. In commanding him to repent, Christ calls upon him to look back as he thinks.

As we look back and think, we shall see what we once were in Adam—children of God, meant to live in eternal fellowship with Him, without sin and its consequences. As we reflect upon what we were, we are made conscious of the difference between that state and what we are now. And we see that the greatest loss man has ever suffered is the marring of God's image in him. From being children of God we became children of the devil. That is why the Lord Jesus told the unbelieving people of His day, "Ye are of your father the devil, and the lusts of your father ye will do" (John 8:44). What a calamity we have brought upon ourselves by voluntarily exchanging God for the devil as our father! No wonder we are in such a mess. We failed to exercise forethought, and the only alternative open to us now is afterthought.

To think back and to discover that we are not what we were meant to be and therefore are unhappy does not help us much. Here is someone who has fallen from a great precipice. He realizes he is lost, he is not where he ought to be, but what good does that do him? There are two alternatives for a man in such a predicament. One is to try to help himself out of his lost condition. The other is to cry for help from someone else. Most people follow their natural inclinations by trying to do the first. We have the instinct of self-preservation.

When we realize we are lost, we endeavor to find a way out. This is what is advocated by most preachers and most religions. This is a help-yourself, save-yourself style of religion. But it concerns itself only with the present and the future. We may determine to do differently now and hereafter. But we must not forget that "to repent" in Greek means to have afterthoughts, nor forethoughts. It is to recollect our failures before God. We cannot act as though we have merely the present and the future to reckon with, for we carry over a debt from the past.

Billy Sunday once told of a man who came to him and said, "I'll cut out the booze and get on the water wagon." "Good; what else?" "I guess I'll quit cussing." "All right; what else?" "Of course, I'm a gambler; I'll quit gambling and I'll never touch a pack of cards." "All right; what else?" "I'm a bad man, and I'll live a clean life." "Good; what else?" He said, "If I quit these things, I think they cover about all. I'll quit drinking, swearing, stop gambling, and I'll quit being impure." Billy said, "Good. Give me your hand and say you'll accept Jesus Christ as your Saviour." He said, "No, I won't. If I stop those things, I won't need to do that."

Is that really so, or is that just man's way of salvation? Those are simple resolutions. Resolutions have to do with the present and the future, but they cannot affect the past. Supposing you owed a man twenty-five dollars and you should go to him and say, "I've made up my mind that I'm going to pay cash for what I get from now on." "Good; I'm glad of that resolution. But you owe me twenty-five dollars; what about that?" "Oh, if I pay cash from now on that will make us square." No, resolutions to reform are not what Jesus meant by the command to repent. Repentance involves an afterthought of the past. And anyone who is honest with himself will recognize that his past is not sinless. The Bible definitely tells us this. "For all have sinned," we read in Romans 3:23. And the Psalmist says, "They are all gone aside, they are all together become filthy: there is none that doeth good, no, not one" (Ps. 14:3).

Now the Bible declares that in order for past sins to be cleared, blood must be shed: for "without shedding of blood is no remission" (Heb. 9:22). Your blood and mine could not atone for sin. Only the blood of a sinless and perfect individual could do that. Such was Jesus Christ—God who became man that He might die in order for men to live.

What Christ is asking you to do by commanding you to repent is to stop and think, think back, think of your past sinfulness, inherited and personal. He then asks you to realize that there is absolutely nothing you can do to help yourself in eradicating that sin, the sin of Adam as your federal representative, as well as your own sins. Continue to think back and look back. You will come to see that the Lord Jesus Christ died for you so that your past might be clear and your future bright. To reject such an opportunity would be spiritual suicide. But it is only as you look back to the cross of Calvary, where Christ died for you, that your future can become bright and hopefully certain. Only as you experience forgiveness for sin can you have victory over sin.

Thus, to repent means to look back and realize you are lost, that you cannot save yourself, and that the only One who can save you is the One who paid the only acceptable penalty for sin, the shedding of His blood—the Lord Jesus Christ. The Apostle Peter declared it in unmistakable words when he referred to the exclusiveness of Christ as Saviour in Acts 4:12: "Neither is there salvation in any other: for there is none other name under heaven given among men, whereby we must be saved."

The recognition of your sinful and lost estate does not necessarily mean that you have to understand fully how and why it all happened before you can cry out for help and salvation. A man once came to a preacher and asked, "How is it that I was born with an evil heart? Is that fair, that I should inherit the sin of Adam?" The preacher replied, "That's a question which does not concern you so much as another, namely, how to get rid of your evil heart. You have an evil heart which renders you completely unfit for the Kingdom of God; and you must have a new heart or you cannot be saved; and the question which now most deeply concerns you is, how shall you obtain it?" But the man insisted, "I wish you would tell me how I came by my wicked heart." "I shall not do that at present," replied the preacher, "for if I could do it to your entire satisfaction, it would not in the least help you toward obtaining a new heart. The great thing for which I am desirous is that you should become a new creature and be prepared for heaven." Then he continued, "You are like a man who is drowning. Along come his friends to save him, but he insists on being told exactly how he came to be drowning before he will consent to be rescued." The man started to think. The preacher was right. The most urgent thing for him and for you is not the full understanding of why and how you came to be what you are, but to rush to the Saviour, to become what you can be—a child of God by receiving Jesus Christ. This is what it means to repent, to realize your lost condition and to rush to the shelter of salvation, to go to Christ.

SORROW FOR THE PAST BRINGS HOPE FOR THE FUTURE

Thinking of the past, we are told by some, is not always the most healthy thing to do. It will bring us face to face with too many of our failures and disappointments, our sad and lamentable experiences. So we are advised to try to forget the past.

Memory, however, should not be considered a curse. It is really a blessing. It is a reality, and realities have to be faced instead of being evaded. "Memory," Basile said, "is the cabinet of imagination, the treasury of reason, the registry of conscience, and the council chamber of thought." When the Lord Jesus commanded all men to repent, He asked them among other things to exercise their memories: for as we saw previously in our study, the word *metanoeoo* in Greek, "to repent," actually means "to think after," to have afterthoughts about our lives.

It is true that there is also an element of sorrow that arises as a result of this afterthought or the exercise of memory. When the Lord Jesus commands us to look back by saying *metanoeite,* "repent," He indicates that this will produce sorrow in us. This is the sorrow that comes from the discovery of our lost condition. A person who is dying is not happy; a person who is drowning is not singing. We find out we are lost and undone, and the natural reaction is sorrow. This is as it should be according to the Scriptures. Repentance that is not followed by deep sorrow of heart can hardly be called repentance. The Greek word *metanoia* definitely involves sorrow. The Scriptures tells us how we should come to God after realizing our sinfulness as a consequence of looking back at our lives. "Turn ye even to me with all your heart, and with fasting, and with weeping, and with mourning" (Joel 2:12). "The Lord is nigh unto them that are of a broken heart; and saveth such as be of a contrite spirit" (Ps. 34:18). David realized that sorrow was involved in repentance when he said in one of his prayers. "The sacrifices of God are a broken spirit: a broken and a contrite heart, O God, thou wilt not despise" (Ps. 51:17).

A story is told of Origen, one of the most distinguished of all theologians (A.D. 185-254), who had fallen into serious backsliding and then somewhat recovered from it. Coming into a congregation, he was desired to preach. He took the Bible and opened it accidentally at the Fiftieth Psalm, when his eyes fell on these words in the 16th and 17th verses: "But unto the wicked God saith, What hast thou to do to declare my statutes, or that thou shouldest take my covenant in thy mouth? Seeing thou hatest instruction, and casteth my words behind thee." Upon reading these words, he remembered his own fall, and instead of preaching he fell to weeping and wept so bitterly that he caused all the congregation to weep with him. How we need such preaching and preachers today, who both preach repentance and practice it—those who sorrow for their own sins and for the sins of others. Repentance does not involve laughter but tears as we pensively view our lives in retrospect. This is sorrow to be desired, "For godly sorrow worketh repentance to salvation not to be repented of: but the sorrow of the world worketh death" (II Cor. 7:10). Godly sorrow is sorrow for sin, and worldly sorrow is sorrow because of sin.

In our English versions there are two Greek verbs which are translated by the same word "repent." These, however, must be distinguished. They are *metanoeoo,* used in Matthew 4:17, which constitutes the commandment of Christ under study, and *metamelomai.* The substantive of the verb *metamelomai* (*metameleia*) is never used in the New Testament. But the substantive of the first verb, *metanoeoo,* is used extensively. What is the difference between these two Greek verbs? Let us consider *metamelomai,* which is not the verb used in Matthew 4:17. It signifies either the beginning of a good repentance or the whole state of an ineffective repentance. Take Matthew 21:32, for instance. After the Lord gave the parable of the two sons, He said, "For John came unto you in the way of righteousness, and ye believed him not: but the publicans and the harlots believed him: and ye, when ye had seen it, repented not [*metemeleetheete*] afterward, that ye might believe him." Here we find that these people did not make the good beginning toward believing.

And then we have Judas. He changed his mind and returned the thirty pieces of silver, but that does not mean that he really repented. The word used in the Greek is *metameleetheis.* "Then Judas, which had betrayed him, when he saw that he was condemned, repented [*metameleetheis*] himself, and brought again the thirty pieces of silver to the chief priests and elders" (Matt. 27:3). And yet we find afterward that he went out and committed suicide. This was an ineffective repentance. Therefore this verb *metamelomai* (occurring in Matt. 21:29, 32; 27:3; II Cor. 7:8, and Heb. 7:21) means either the beginning of a good repentance or the whole state of an ineffective repentance.

That *metanoia* is the better word in the New Testament is demonstrated by the use the Apostle Paul makes of the two words in one verse. II Corinthians 7:10, which reads, "For godly sorrow worketh repentance [*metanoian*] to salvation not to be repented of [*ametameleeton,* the adjective of the verb *metamelomai*]: but the sorrow of the world worketh death." What Paul is declaring here is that real repentance involves godly sorrow, that is, sorrow for our sins, and that once we repent we shall never regret it. Thus the word "repentance," *metanoia,* means the effectual transformation of a person, and the verb *metamelomai,* here given in its adjectival form, means mere regret. A man can be sorry about his past life and yet have no desire either to be forgiven or to live a new life, free from willful sin. Judas was sorry but he did not really repent of his sin. Had he repented, he would not have hanged himself.

Thus, to focus the meaning of repentance, *metanoia,* as predominantly used in the New Testament, involves the following steps. As we enumerate these steps, however, we should make clear that the process of repentance and salvation is so unified that the person who experiences it is often not fully conscious of the steps taken and the order in which they occur, although it is beneficial to know what they are. Here, then, is what a Christian who has repented has come through:

1. A reckoning with the past. The one who repents must look back, must give afterthought to his life, recognizing that it is sinful. He must realize that he is lost and without hope of saving himself, that he needs help from outside himself, from the Lord Jesus Christ, who is the only qualified Saviour.

2. A change of mind. The one who repents must realize that he is lost, that his past is sinful, and determine in his mind to be found, to be forgiven, and resolve once he is forgiven and found not to fall into the same trap again. He makes a judgment about the past and determination about a new frontier of blessed fellowship with God and all that is good.

3. Contrition of heart. Repentance is not only looking back and changing one's mind about the present and the future, but also sorrowing for the past sinful life.

4. A change of conduct. Finally, if a man has his eyes fixed on the sinful past, has changed his mind about it, and is sorry for it, he will change his

actions to square with his beliefs. This is proof that his change of mind is not theoretical but practical. Belief that is not interpreted in behavior is not belief at all. In pre-New Testament times, "repentance" could be a change for the better or for the worse. It is after the use of the word in the New Testament that *metanoia,* "repentance," came to acquire an ethical sense, signifying a change for the better and not for the worse.

5. Turning over the controls to God. Repentance in its full development in the New Testament signifies the miraculous working of the Holy Spirit in the heart, mind, and life of an individual, changing his entire viewpoint toward life and giving him God's nature within. Repentance in the New Testament does not simply involve a change of mind and heart, but it involves man's placing himself at the disposal of the Holy Spirit to work in him the miracles of conversion, of inner change of personality and life and its consequent outward manifestation. Man in faith invites Jesus Christ, the Saviour, to come into his heart and life, and Christ does just that. Repentance is not mere conviction. It is one thing for a man to be awakened at five o'clock in the morning and it is another thing for him to get up. When the prodigal son realized his lost condition, he got up and went back to his father; and the father accepted him.

FALSE AND TRUE REPENTANCE

In order that repentance may result in the remission of sins, it must be genuine. By what criteria do we determine whether the repentance of a certain individual is true or false? Some people who think they repent are disappointed because they do not subsequently experience the knowledge of sin forgiven. The result is frustration. What is the use of repenting if the outcome is not what is expected and what is promised in the Word of God? That is why it is important for us to think seriously, first about false repentance and then about true repentance.

Men may mistake mere sorrow over sins for repentance. Having come to the conclusion that their deeds are sinful, they go so far as to confess their sins and feel humbled for them. And yet it is quite possible for them to do all this and yet not to evidence true repentance.

You remember how Moses tried to persuade Pharaoh to let the children of Israel leave the bondage of Egypt, but he refused. Then Moses invoked a number of plagues upon Egypt. It was after the plague of hailstones that Pharoah sent for Moses and Aaron and confessed, "I have sinned this time: the Lord is righteous, and I and my people are wicked" (Exod. 9:27). Was this repentance? Not at all. A mere confession of sin does not represent repentance.

We find the same confession of sin coming from the lips of Balaam (Numbers 22:34), Saul (I Sam. 15:24), and even Judas, who having betrayed his Master confessed, "I have sinned in that I have betrayed the innocent blood" (Matt. 27:4). These men confessed particular sins in their lives of which they were convinced and convicted, yet they did not receive forgiveness, for their repentance was not genuine. Theirs was a convenient confession of the mouth not springing from a belief of heart. "For with the heart," says the Apostle Paul, "man believeth unto righteousness; and with the mouth confession is made unto salvation" (Rom. 10:10).

Genuine repentance involves a change in the inward state of man. It has nothing to do with the body. It is all in the seat of thought and disposition. It involves a complete transformation of man. It is not mere conviction of sins, but conviction of sinfulness. Repentance involves the mind and heart and produces an aversion to the evil of which we feel convicted.

Furthermore, it is possible for a person even to give up many of the sins of which he was previously guilty and yet not really repent. It is possible, in other words, for a man's deeds and conversation to be changed while his mind and heart remain unaltered. You cannot change a tree, or kill its roots, by lopping off some of its branches or hacking at the trunk. You may have quit certain sins of the past, but does that mean that you have repented of those sins? Not unless the root responsible for the growth of those sins has been torn out. Haven't you heard people say, "I wish I could do certain things, but my hands are tied"? Many of us do not do things, not because we don't want to do them, but because we cannot do them; we are afraid to do them. A person who has lived an immoral life for a long time may finally settle down. He no longer engages in acts of immorality, but deep in his heart he wishes he could. We have not truly repented of a certain sin if we would repeat it if we could. If we are sorry at being deprived of the pleasures of sin, or give them up for any other reason than their sinfulness, then our sorrow is not real repentance.

Let us take a concrete illustration. Here is a rich person who at present is scrupulously honest. He has reached the place where he does not engage in any shady business. And yet in his younger days he used all kinds of trickery and unlawful means to acquire his wealth. Oh, yes, he is honest now, but he is enjoying the wealth that he acquired by dishonesty. His present honesty does not spring from real repentance over his past dishonesty, but rather from the fact that he no longer needs to be dishonest to satisfy himself. If he needed to, it is quite possible that he would once again employ trickery to acquire wealth. It is false repentance which enables us to enjoy the pleasant results of past sin, in spite of the fact that we may vehemently denounce such sin. We no longer commit it because we don't need to, but if we had to in order to acquire what we now enjoy, we would not hesitate to engage in a repeat performance. That is false repentance. Let us examine ourselves carefully to determine whether what we thought to be real repentance for sin was simply a convenient change of policy, based not on our conviction of the sinfulness of sin but on expediency in the face of changed circumstances. Our lives may be reformed yet our hearts still be sinful. Repentance, genuine repentance, does not involve the mere giving up of sins but ceasing to be sinful. What we need is not a change of acts and words but a change of hearts and minds. That is actually what *metanoia*—"repentance"—means. As Bishop Beveridge says, "Do but clean the fountain, and the streams will soon run clear. But never think that you have repented of any sin, merely because you do not commit it now, as heretofore you used to do; but rather consider which way your pulse beats, and whether your hearts be still inclined to it or no, and whether you find your hearts so changed from it, that you hate it now as much as ever you loved it; that you abhor it now as much as ever you did desire it, and that you are as really grieved for it now, as ever heretofore you took pleasure in it. And until you find such an alteration in your minds, let no alteration whatsoever in your lives fool you into a groundless persuasion, that you have repented: for I assure you, you have not." (*The Works of Bishop William Beveridge,* Vol. IV, p. 514)

Is your repentance genuine or false? Since repentance involves thought, serious thought, afterthought, it is good to have some afterthoughts about what you may superficially have taken to be repentance in your life. Rethink your thoughts about repentance. It involves your present happiness and your eternal destiny.

You recall how Elijah the prophet had convinced Ahab of his sins. Ahab and his wife Jezebel were indeed evil people. Of Ahab, the Word of God says, "But there was none like unto Ahab, which did sell himself to work wickedness in the sight of the Lord whom Jezebel his wife stirred up" (I Kings 21:25). Ahab was told by Elijah of the judgments of God that would come upon him for his sins. And what was Ahab's response to that? "And it came to pass, when Ahab heard those words, that he rent his clothes, and put sackcloth upon his flesh, and fasted, and lay in sackcloth" (I Kings 21:27). This was penance, self-imposed. But there is no indication at all that Ahab was in any way changed, or that his sins were forgiven. In spite of the conviction that he had sinned, in spite of his fasting and humiliation, his was not a genuine repentance. What actually troubled Ahab was the threat of the judgments of God upon him. He was not concerned about the sins he had committed against God but about the consequences of his sins. He was like the criminal who, when convicted of his crimes, confesses them but would repeat them if the opportunity arose. The motive and not the act of repentance is what determines whether it is genuine. When my little boy does something wrong, I scold him and call him to repentance. I invite him, it may be, to turn to his sister whom he has struck and ask her pardon. He says,

"Lois, I am sorry." Now is this repentance? It all depends on his motive. Did he say, "I am sorry," because he was afraid of punishment from his father or reprisals from his sister; or was it because he thought by saying it he would be rewarded? Or was it because he realized the wrong of what he had done? Repentance to be genuine must be characterized by purity of motive. It must not be motivated purely and basically by the fear of punishment or the hope of reward. Sin must be condemned because it is sin. And only when this happens is it least likely to be repeated.

As Bishop Beveridge says again, "If whipping our bodies would save our souls, or scourging our backs would mortify our sins, or going barefoot was the way to go to heaven, none but fools and madmen would be kept out; nothing being more easy than to perform such external actions out of pride or hypocrisy, and yet continue in sin still."

IS REPENTANCE A ONE-TIME THING?

In Matthew 3:2 we read that, when John the Baptist began his ministry in the desert, the burden of his preaching was "Repent ye: for the kingdom of heaven is at hand." In the Greek, the word is the imperative *metanoeite,* "repent ye." It was a commandment.

Then along comes the Lord Jesus Christ, and in Matthew 4:17 we find Him repeating exactly the same commandment, "*Metanoeite,* repent ye." Why? Did not the Lord Jesus have a different message from that of John the Baptist? Did He have nothing new to add?

We believe the Lord had several reasons for repeating this commandment:

1. To show that a good and necessary commandment is worth repeating. People then did not like to hear this message of repentance any better than they do today. It presupposed that they were sinners, and they did not like that. People then and now like to hear, not what they need, but what they like.

A church in need of a pastor called a candidate to preach for several consecutive Sundays. The first Sunday he preached on man's sinfulness, calling on sinners to repent. At the end of the service one of the elders cornered the preacher and said to him, "If that is what you are going to be preaching to us, we don't want you. We don't want to hear how bad we are, but how good we are." Needless to say, this faithful young preacher did not receive a call to that church. In line with Christ's example, His first message was "Repent ye." He did not consider it outdated, for there are always sinners who need this first commandment of Christ.

What would happen to a sick person if the doctor gave him only what he liked and not what he needed? Christ preached what people needed, even if it was a repetition of the message of His predecessor, John the Baptist. How we need preachers who preach what people need, salvation in Christ!

A young minister in a college town was embarrassed by the thought of criticism from his cultured congregation. He sought counsel from his father, a wise old minister, saying, "Dad, I am handicapped in my ministry in the pulpit I am now serving. If I cite anything from geology, there is Prof. A—, teacher of this science, right before me. If I use an illustration from Roman mythology, there is Prof. B— ready to trip me up for any little inaccuracy. If I mention something in English literature that pleases me, I am cowered by the presence of the learned man that teaches that branch. What shall I do?" The sagacious old man replied, "Do not be discouraged; preach the Gospel. They probably know very little of that." How true.

2. To confirm what His prophets, including His forerunner John the Baptist, had preached. He was the climax and fulfillment of their preaching. He did not come to put an end to it but to confirm and supplement it. In Ezekiel 14:6 we read, "Therefore say unto the house of Israel, Thus saith the Lord God; Repent, and turn yourselves from your idols; and turn away your faces from all your abominations." In between the Old and New Testaments stands John the Baptist, repeating God's first and last message of repentance. To confirm that this was indeed Christ's message, given in advance of His coming, and that this was to be the message that would follow His advent, our Lord repeated it. Then, just before He departed from this earth, He told His disciples to preach the same message. We find this in Luke 24:47: "And that repentance and remission of sins should be preached in his name among all nations, beginning at Jerusalem." Let us not, therefore, reject or minimize what the pre-incarnate

Word said through His prophets, for in His incarnation He repeated their message, a message that had pointed to Him as the fulfillment of God's plan for the ages.

3. To show that repentance has always been and still is God's first commandment to man. There is to this day a shallow concept in many circles that the God of the New Testament is quite different from the God of the Old Testament, that the one is an austere and cruel God, and the other a God of love who will never punish anyone but will ultimately save everyone and enable all to live a life of everlasting bliss. But if we think about it a few moments, we shall see that this first commandment of Christ's for everyone to repent is indeed His diagnosis of the condition of man—that he is utterly lost and completely depraved. Otherwise His message would not have been "Repent" but "Develop that divine spark that is in you." The God of the Old Testament treated man as a sinner, and the God of the Old Testament treats him exactly the same way. The message of the Old Testament was Repent, and that of John the Baptist was Repent; that of Christ's apostles was Repent; and ours should be Repent. That is because man is a sinner. Because he has become civilized, that does not mean that he has ceased to be sinful.

A story is told of a clergyman who had just been called to a wealthy church. Wanting to present the facts of the Gospel to them tactfully, without hurting anyone's feelings, he said, "You should repent, to some extent; or else you might be damned, more or less; and possibly go to hell, in a measure." By inviting men to repent, Christ made it evident that they were sinners and that they needed salvation. He who could read the minds and hearts of men better than anyone could certainly diagnose their ailment. Christ said, "I tell you, Nay: but, except ye repent, ye shall all likewise perish (Luke 13:3).

Very interestingly, this verb *metanoeite,* "repent," is in the present imperative, which indicates that this repentance was not only to have a starting point but that it was to continue constantly and uninterruptedly. Repentance is not a once-and-for-all experience but should be a repeated one in the life of sinful man. Jesus Christ did not summon people to repent once and for all, but to turn from their ways and unto God, fully recognizing that their lives would always be characterized by imperfections and sins from which they would have the opportunity, and were called upon, to repent.

No man can live a perfect life. Even after his conversion he needs to repent of his ways. What the Lord Jesus commands us to do is keep on repenting even after we accept Him as our Saviour and Lord. Even as Christians, dare we claim that we have done our best for Him? It was Spurgeon who wisely said, "He who boasts of being perfect is perfect in folly. I never saw a perfect man. Every rose has its thorns, and every day its night. Even the sun shows spots, and the skies are darkened with clouds. And faults of some kind nestle in every bosom."

In view of our imperfect state, even after repenting once of our originial and personal sin, let us keep on repenting. That's what Christ commands us to do. The Christian life is a life of not only one repentance but of many repentances. Although we are born just once into the family of God, as members of that family we often stand in need of forgiveness.

IS IT POSSIBLE TO FALL AGAIN INTO THE SINS WE HAVE REPENTED OF?

In our last study we called attention to the fact that the commandment to repent as given to us by John the Baptist and by the Lord Jesus Christ is *metanoeite,* which involves a continuous repentance. In Mark 1:4 we read that John the Baptist preached the baptism of repentance for the remission of sins. What we are told is that, if we repent of certain sins, they will be forgiven us. But the big question that emerges is this: Is it possible to fall again into the sins of which we have once repented and for which we have been forgiven?

In the first place, we find in the New Testament that the Christian is enjoined to forgive his brother not merely seven times, as Peter suggested, but seventy times seven—in other words, *ad infinitum.* The fact that we have to forgive our brother as often as he offends us indicates that our brother can fall into sin, and possibly the same sin, many times. Would God be less willing to forgive than He expects us to be? Inconceivable. When Christ commands us to repent—time and time again—He surely presupposes His willingness and readiness to forgive us each time. But this by no means should be looked upon as an encouragement to sin. In spite of the fact that the Christian may sin, repent, and be forgiven many times over in the course of his life, it is impossible for him to find pleasure in such sin. If a so-called Christian does, he has never experienced the grace of God; he has never experienced the initial repentance which marks that initial and basic forgiveness and entry into the family of God.

The first argument in support of these facts is the tense in which the commandment is given us—*metanoeite,* "continuously repent," keep on repenting for the remission of your sins. Since we must keep on repenting, the possibility exists that there will be a repetition of the sins of which we repent. Now we do not advocate such a repetition, nor do we say that there is pleasure in it, or that such repetition is inevitable. But we must face the fact that it is possible, with a varying degree of probability depending on our state of yieldedness to Jesus Christ.

When we repent and our hearts and minds are changed, our faces, so to speak, are turned toward God and our backs toward sin. But sin does not disappear from the world in which we live. It is ever present; and although we run away from it, of one thing we can be sure—it will always be at our heels. A converted, saved person is one who runs away from sin, never one who delights in sin. Yet that change which occurs in us when we initially repent is not an absolutely perfect change. We do not get rid of our Adamic nature and therefore we are not delivered from all possibility of sin. David was certainly a dear saint of God, and yet he committed sins which make us tremble even as we think of them. Peter surely loved the Lord, but under pressure of adverse circumstances, while his Lord was being tried inside, he kept company with His enemies in the courtyard and not only denied Him but reinforced his denial with oaths and curses. This in spite of the fact that he had previously asserted he would never do so. Boastfully he had said, "Though I should die with thee, yet will I not deny thee" (Matt. 26:35). And yet he did. Why? Because he was still a man, an imperfect man. But even when the sin of which we have truly repented recurs, it is not enthroned as king, but is considered a tyrant and a usurper. A man with a regenerate heart truly hates the evil which he once loved and truly loves the good which he once hated.

But repentance, genuine repentance, does not result merely in aversion to sin but has a positive side also. It achieves not only victory over evil but the performance of good. There are duties consequent upon repentance. When we truly repent, we not only avoid that which displeases God, but we also do those things which please Him. We not only hate evil, but love good. We not only refrain from stealing, but we help others. We not only avoid adultery, but contribute for the care of those who but for our charity would be tempted to sin. Not only should we not lie, but proclaim the truth and expose falsehood. The greatest victory over sin comes to the man who has turned his eyes toward God and, though he does not worry about the possibility of sin overcoming him, is nevertheless prepared to face it. Peter, when summoned by his Lord to walk on the waters, was doing all right until he took his eyes off the Lord and centered them on the waves. A safe rule after repentance is not to look back upon the sins from which we have been freed, but to look upon Christ who has freed us. "Let the wicked forsake his way, and the unrighteous man his thoughts: and let him return unto the Lord" (Isaiah 55:7). And the prophet Joel says, "Rend your heart, and not your garments, and turn unto the Lord your God" (2:13).

This commandment, *metanoeite,* "repent," in the Greek is not only in the present imperative, which indicates continuous repentance from sin, but it is also in the active voice, which indicates a voluntary act of man's. Repentance is not something imposed upon us by God but is something that we decide upon for ourselves. The Lord calls us to repentance, but He does not force it upon us. If repentance were not voluntary, it would be like the imprisonment of a criminal in a cell. While he was free he could steal, but now that he is in prison he must refrain. That does not mean that he is honest. If repentance were forced upon us, it would not bring us the joy of the Lord but only the fear of the Lord. If we repent by our own choice, we shall be happy indeed. In fact the only way we *can* be happy is to repent of our sins and turn our eyes upon Jesus Christ. If we refuse truly to repent, we incur the penalty of our own sin. No man must blame God for sending him to hell. He permits himself to go there because of his refusal to repent and go to heaven. Actually in his choice lie his eternal happiness and salvation or his eternal damnation. God sends no one to hell. Those go there who refuse to repent.

Very interestingly the Apostle Paul says, "The goodness of God leadeth thee to repentance" (Rom. 2:4). Although the active choice is man's, there is a leading, and energizing of the Spirit of God unto repentance without which man would choose to remain away from God and in his sin. God has no selfish purpose in inviting us to repent. His invitation is motivated by His goodness, mercy, and grace. He is happy in Himself. Your repentance and mine do not primarily determine God's happiness but our own happiness and blessedness. Of course, God experiences sorrow over our refusal to repent and joy over our repentance, but this does not affect His eternal character—only the expression of His character. He weeps and laughs. But these actions do not determine what He is, for what one does is the result and not the cause of what one is. The glory of God is not darkened by our misery, nor is it advanced by our happiness. Whatever God does for us, including His leading us to repent, is not for His benefit but for ours. If we could only grasp this eternal truth, how much more willingly we would accept God's dealing with us. Ezekiel says, "As I live, saith the Lord, I have no pleasure in the death of the wicked; but that the wicked turn from his way and live: turn ye, turn ye from your evil ways; for why will ye die, O house of Israel?" (Ezek. 33:11).

The importance of a command is determined by

who gives it. A command given by one of my children to the other does not carry much weight. But when I as a parent issue a command, the matter is much different. A soldier dare not disobey a command given by his superior officer, but he does not pay much attention to one given by a fellow soldier of the same rank. Here we have the command to repent given not only by John the Baptist but by the Lord Jesus Himself. It is He who made the world, He who made you, the God of heaven come down to earth, who says to you, "Repent." It is One who knows your need because He became man to experience it for Himself. It is the One who died for your sins and knows how terrible is the penalty of sin. In fact, He is the only One who understands the horrible implications of sin, and because of His understanding of sin and its implications He calls us to repentance. By His sufferings He made a way for us to repent, and by this commandment He is directing us how to walk in that way to heaven. The reason why He is so concerned that we repent is that if we do not we shall perish (Luke 13:3). If there were any other way by which we could receive remission of sins and attain happiness and heaven, He would have told us. But it is certain that the only gate to happiness and Heaven is repentance. Have you truly repented? Have you turned to Christ?

WHAT SHOULD BE THE MOTIVE OF REPENTANCE?

In order to understand the true meaning and implications of repentance, we must examine the commandment of Christ not only as given to us by Matthew but as recorded by Mark. Of the four Gospels, Mark's was written first and is considered basic. Mark was a nephew of Barnabas, the fellow traveler of the Apostle Paul on his first missionary journey, and, despite the rift that occurred between them at one time, he was still one of his closest associates during the last days of his life. (See Acts 12: 12, 25; 13:13; 15:37-40; Col. 4:10; II Tim. 4:11). It would seem that Mark's record of the life of Jesus Christ was based on Peter's preaching, for Peter himself calls him "Marcus my son" (I Pet. 5:13). It is also noteworthy that, of Mark's 661 verses, Matthew reproduces 606 and Luke 320. Therefore we may conclude that Matthew, in recording this first commandment of Christ, consulted Mark, who gave it more fully as follows: "The time is fulfilled, and the kingdom of God is at hand: repent ye, and believe the gospel" (Mark 1:15). Matthew simply says, "Repent ye: for the kingdom of heaven is at hand" (3:2).

Matthew records the preaching of John the Baptist as being identical with that of the Lord Jesus Christ. "In those days came John the Baptist, preaching in the wilderness of Judaea, and saying, Repent ye: for the kingdom of heaven is at hand" (Matt. 3:1, 2). But Mark's version of the preaching of John the Baptist is different—more explicit—even as is his statement concerning the preaching of Christ. "John did baptize in the wilderness, and preach the baptism of repentance for the remission of sins" (Mark 1:4).

In comparing these verses referring to the preaching of both John the Baptist and the Lord Jesus, it is apparent that Mark qualifies and expounds the commandment to repent. In the case of John's preaching he adds (1) the element of baptism and (2) the element of the remission of sins. In the case of Christ's preaching he adds (1) that the time is fulfilled and (2) that repentance is to be accompanied by belief in the Gospel. We shall do well to examine these additions of Mark, which Matthew did not mention in his record, for they will shed light on what Christ meant by His commandment to repent.

Mark very vividly presents our Lord not only as Christ or God but also as Jesus the man, manifesting great compassion to man, His creature. The human and benevolent Jesus stands out all through the Gospel of Mark. As man, the Lord Jesus fully understood the misery of man under the dominion of sin. The greatest burden that man was and is carrying is sin—the sin of Adam and his own personal sin. Sin makes man miserable, robs life of its worth and joy. Since the primary purpose of Jesus Christ is to restore happiness to man, and since happiness is only possible as man is connected with the source of happiness, God his Creator, and since sin is the only thing that separates man from God, Jesus Christ came to remove the cause of this separation and unhappiness. Therefore Mark declares the purpose of repentance as being "the remission of sins." That should be the only motive of repentance. The Christian should refrain from sin because of its sinfulness and not because of its consequences.

There is no doubt that people like to sin but they dislike the consequences of their sins. A man likes to drink but he dislikes being drunk and all that goes with it. And people are consciously or unconsciously afraid of the consequences of sin. We find this vividly portrayed in the actions of many of the Jews who came to John the Baptist for baptism, without first having repented. They thought water baptism an easy way of being freed from the consequences of their sins; so they came to John in droves, misunderstanding what he was doing. They thought that his "baptism of repentance" merely meant baptism that took the place of repentance. How caustically John rebuked them: "O generation of vipers, who hath warned you to flee from the wrath to come?" (Luke 3:7). That is all they were doing—fleeing from the wrath to come, fleeing from the consequences of their sins. This is a wrong motive either for baptism or for repentance.

Now why does the Gospel of Mark explain the motive of repentance as being the remission of man's sins? Because there is a kind of false repentance which simply involves sorrow for the consequences of sin rather than for sin itself. Let us say that a person steals and is caught. The consequence of his sin is imprisonment and a damaged reputation. As long as he could sin without detection, he had no compunction about his sin. He is sorry now, of course, but only because he has been caught and is suffering the consequences of his sin. While he is in jail, a Christian worker witnesses to him. As a result he says, "I will repent, if that is the only way I can keep out of jail." But if that is what motivates his repentance, he will most probably be released only to steal again—once more in the hope that he will not suffer the consequences of his sin. Or if he refrains from sinning simply because he is afraid of the consequences, that does not mean that he is a child of God, a Christian who has experienced forgiveness of sin; he is just trying to avoid punishment for sin.

Our world is full of such people, and that is why the law was instituted. But grace, the grace of God, does something far more radical than act as a deterrent on the one who really repents because of his sorrow at offending God his Creator. It places God within his heart, the One who abhors sin; so that sin itself becomes repulsive to him, rather than the mere consequences of sin. We should be careful to distinguish between the genuine repentance which is preached by Christ and the repentance which results from fear of the law and its punishment. Look deep in your heart and see what kind of repentance you have exercised. Is it repentance because of sin or merely because of the consequences of sin?

Now there are those who will try to read into this statement of Mark, concerning the preaching of John the Baptist, support for their view that remission of sins is effected as a result of baptism. We believe this to be erroneous. John did not preach baptism for the remission of sins, but the baptism of repentance for the remission of sins. There is a difference. What was the purpose of baptism in the Old Testament? Chapters 11 through 15 of Leviticus describe the ritual washings which were the baptism of the Old Testament. Washing is symbolic of cleanliness and implies that a person must first realize that he is dirty. The Jews realized that they were defiled daily and therefore needed these daily washings. And then consider the procedure for the Gentile when he became a proselyte, a convert to the Jewish faith. He had to be circumcised, because that brought him into the family of God's covenant people. Then a blood sacrifice had to be made for his atonement, for the Jews believed that only through the shedding of blood could there be remission of sin. And finally he had to be baptized as a testimony that he had been cleansed from his past sin.

Now John the Baptist was preaching primarily to Jews, who already had their daily ablutions or baptisms. Only the Gentiles had to be instructed to be baptized, for the Jews were baptized daily. But John invites Jews like himself to undergo a different kind of baptism, the baptism of repentance, which was qualitatively different from that which they experienced so frequently in obedience to the Levitical law. Even the chosen people of God, with Christ's public ministry now impending, needed something more, even as did the Gentiles; and that was the baptism of repentance. Constant sacrifices and daily baptism for their sins were no longer necessary. The atonement of the Son of God was at hand and those who appropriated it needed to testify to their cleansing only once. Baptism was to be an outward testimony of something that had happened within their hearts, absolution from sin.

If the Jews, who were considered the chosen people of God, needed to repent, we must conclude that no matter how saintly or "chosen" the national or religious group to which we belong, we need individual repentance. Each of us needs to repent whether we be Jew or Gentile. Remission of sins is not a corporate thing but an individual responsibility, made actual through repentance.

But is the emphasis on repentance or baptism? Which saves—baptism or repentance or both? This we shall see as we study further.

WHAT IS BAPTISM OF REPENTANCE?

Mark presents John the Baptist as preaching the baptism of repentance. He says, "John did baptize in the wilderness and preach the baptism of repentance for the remission of sins" (Mark 1:4). And Luke writes, "And he came into all the country about Jordan, preaching the baptism of repentance for the remission of sins" (Luke 3:3). Since some claim that remission of sins is achieved through repentance and others claim it is through baptism, we must examine these verses very carefully in the original Greek text.

Probably the reason why Matthew, who wrote after Mark, left out the reference to baptism given by Mark was to avoid this very misunderstanding—that baptism had anything to do with the remission of sins. Let us not forget that Matthew used the Gospel of Mark as a reference work when he was writing his Gospel. There are only 55 verses of Mark which Matthew does not reproduce.

What does this "baptism of repentance" mean? In Greek it is *baptisma metanoias,* the word *metanoias* being in the genitive, which is why it is translated "of repentance." In Greek it is all one word, the genitive being denoted by the suffix. It is significant that John preached "baptism of repentance" and not "repentance of baptism." Why was this?

Metanoias ("of repentance") is an attributive genitive. Grammarian William Edward Jelf says, "The substantive to which an attributive genitive is annexed denotes something caused, created, contained, possessed by, dependent on, or a part of the person or thing signified by the attributive genitive." (*A Grammar of the Greek Language,* Third Edition, Vol. II, Syntax, p. 140. See also A. T. Robertson, *A Grammar of the Greek New Testament,* p. 496.) Let us analyze what this means in this particular case. The substantive is *baptisma,* "baptism." The attributive genitive is *metanoias,* "of repentance." Actually, repentance here refers to a person who repents. What we are told, then, is that the baptism of which John speaks belongs to the person who repents and to no one else. Baptism, the baptism first preached by John and later by the Lord Jesus, is dependent upon the repentance of the individual. Baptism without repentance is sheer mockery. Baptism is an outward recognition of something that has taken place within. It is fully dependent upon and caused by the inward transaction.

A certain man thought that by being immersed he could find salvation. A friend of his had quite a time explaining to him that it was not so. But this man insisted that, as water would purify the body, so water consecrated by a minister or priest would purify the soul. Finally, to demonstrate that baptism did not mean regeneration, the friend decided upon an object lesson. "Here," he said. "I take an ink bottle, cork it tight, put a string round the neck, and drag it through the river. How long will it take to clean out the inside?" The answer was obvious, "You'll never in the world clean it out that way." We must understand once and for all that no outward act will ever cleanse us within. Repentance is an act that takes place within us, while baptism is an outward act that demonstrates to the world what has already happened in our hearts.

Thus, neither John the Baptist nor anyone else in the New Testament speaks of "repentance of baptism" but of "baptism of repentance." Baptism depends upon and is caused by repentance and not vice versa. It does not make sense for the unrepentant to be baptized.

In further substantiation of what we have said about the particular meaning of the attributive genitive *metanoias,* "of repentance," Jelf says, "When two substantives are joined together [as is the case here with baptism and repentance], the one that explains and more accurately defines the other is in the genitive, as it is in the expression of some notion whence the notion of the other substantive sprang" (*Ibid,* p. 199). In other words, *metanoias,* "of repentance," here defines baptism, and baptism springs from repentance, not vice versa. We are not saved because of baptism, but we are baptized as a result of our repentance.

Apparently the Jews who came to John the Baptist did misunderstand his baptism and its purpose. They thought that baptism was enough to liberate them from their sins. John spared not words in denouncing such candidates for baptism. "Then said he to the multitude that came forth to be baptized of him, O generation of vipers, who hath warned you to flee from the wrath to come? Bring forth therefore fruits worthy of repentance, and begin not to say within yourselves, We have Abraham to our father: for I say unto you, That God is able of these stones to raise up children unto Abraham" (Luke 3:7, 8).

Observe that John told these Jews that they were to bring forth fruits worthy of "repentance," not of "baptism." It was repentance that he was primarily concerned about rather than baptism. Baptism was simply the outward sign of the inward repentance. He also made it very clear that their Jewish ancestry did not in any way entitle them to this baptism without their first repenting.

It is to be noted also that no article appears before either the word *baptisma* or *metanoias.* Mark does not say, "*the* baptism of *the* repentance," or "*the* baptism of repentance," or "baptism of *the* repentance." Why is the article omitted? This is not easy to determine. There is a possibility that the qualitative stress is desired upon the nouns here. (A. T. Robertson, *a Grammar of the Greek New Testament in the Light of Historical Research,* p. 782.) It is not the particular kind of repentance or baptism that is stressed but the fact that repentance occasions baptism.

John was not seeking to put forth a distinctive "brand" of baptism or repentance. He was preaching the same repentance and the same baptism which the Lord Jesus would shortly be preaching. There is only one repentance and one baptism, although there are many who preach it. It was preached by John the Baptist, by Christ Himself, by the Apostles, and by every faithful preacher of the Gospel of Jesus Christ. The variety of preachers did not indicate a variety of baptisms and repentances. This was not *the* baptism of *the* repentance of John the Baptist, but simply "baptism of repentance." It is exactly the same baptism of repentance preached by us today. (Robertson, *Ibid,* p. 782.) We note that in Luke 3:3, as well as in Acts 13:24 and 19:4, the expression is also without the definite article before either word.

In Luke 20:1-7 and Matthew 21:24-27, we find the Lord Jesus Christ asking the chief priests and scribes a question about the authority and heavenly origin of John's baptism. Although they dared not answer, the implication is clear that John's baptism was not of men but from heaven, the same baptism that the Lord Jesus Christ came to preach, the baptism of repentance. And whenever baptism is mentioned in the New Testament, no matter who is referred to as the baptizer, we can always assume that reference is made to the baptism of repentance spoken of here in Mark 1:4 and Luke 3:3.

In Matthew 3:6 we read, "And were baptized of him [John the Baptist] in Jordan, confessing their sins." The baptism of John was consequent to the confession of sins, that is, consequent to repentance.

We recall the conversion of the Philippian jailer, who was so impressed by the miraculous liberation of Paul and Silas from prison that he besought them saying, "What must I do to be saved?" The answer was not "Be baptized" but "Believe on the Lord Jesus Christ, and thou shalt be saved, and thy house." His whole household heard the Word of the Lord, and it can be safely assumed that all of them, presumably of age, believed on the Lord Jesus Christ for whose sake Paul and Silas had been imprisoned. It was after that experience of repentance and belief that these new converts were baptized. (See Acts 16:25-34.)

Therefore the relation between baptism and repentance has been clearly demonstrated. The command of Christ to repent is in full accord with the command of John the Baptist in Mark 1:4 and Luke 3:3. Christ states the first step, the necessary inner transformation of repentance. John the Baptist mentions the outward witness, baptism, which follows as a consequence. Christ may not have mentioned this outward witness of baptism for two reasons:

(1) That He did not consider it necessary for salvation. If it were as important as repentance, He would surely have mentioned it and made it a definite commandment. This is true of both Matthew 4:17 and Mark 1:15.

(2) That the stress John had placed on how different his baptism was from the ordinary and meaningless ablutions of the Old Testament, which involved no actual change of heart, was sufficient, so that Christ had no further need to amplify the difference between Christian baptism and the ritualistic Levitical baptisms.

THE RELATIONSHIP OF REPENTANCE TO FORGIVENESS OF SINS

In Mark 1:4 we read that the baptism of repentance which John the Baptist preached was for the remission of sins. The sum total of the Gospel message is the forgiveness of man. This is the purpose for which Christ came to this world and this is why He died. Repentance is the first step toward the realization of God's plan for us—forgiveness.

It is therefore important for us to examine this expression, "for the remission of sins." But before doing so, let us recollect what we concluded in our last study, that what John the Baptist was actually preaching was not baptism, but repentance which resulted in baptism as an outward demonstration to the world of that which the Spirit of God had done within the hearts of those who repented.

Having examined the relation of baptism to repentance, we must now examine the relation of repentance to the remission of sins. Mark says, "John came, baptizing in the wilderness and preaching baptism of repentance unto remission of sins" (Mark 1:4, literal translation). And when Peter and the other apostles were asked, "Men and brethren, what shall we do?" Peter said, "Repent, and be baptized every one of you in the name of Jesus Christ for the remission of sins" (Acts 2:37, 38). Repentance has to precede baptism; and since baptism is dependent upon repentance and merely an outward demonstration of it, we must logically conclude that the remission of sins is related to the act of repentance and not to its outward manifestation in baptism. And since baptism is the product of repentance and not the cause of it, we must conclude that the first thing which mark 1:4 declares is that remission of sins is related, not to baptism, but to repentance.

Why were the Jews called upon by John to

repent? Why are all men called upon by the Lord Jesus Christ to repent? Since this is the first and foremost commandment of Christ to all men, it must be that it will meet their greatest need. And what is this need? The forgiveness of sins. This, then, indicates that all men are sinners. Sin is the cause of all human unhappiness. Christ wants us to be happy, to be blessed. But in order that we may achieve happiness, the cause of our unhappiness must be removed. This can only come about through repentance. The result of repentance is "remission of sins."

The preposition "for," *eis* in Greek, is used here with a causal or purposive meaning. It indicates the object and purpose of repentance. Man's mental state is one of desperate unhappiness and guilt. He wants to be freed from this guilt of sin and state of unhappiness. He wants to reach, so to speak, the other side of the river. But he cannot discover, by intuition or reflection, how to get across. It is the revelation of God in Christ which provides the necessary bridge, the bridge of repentance, which, if a man crosses will bring him to the other side where he will receive forgiveness and remission of sin.

Thus we see that there was a definite purpose in the preaching of John the Baptist, and of course in the preaching of the Lord Jesus Christ. The commandment is not theoretical but has practical implications for our lives. Unfortunately, so much of the so-called Christian preaching of today is mere philosophy, mere theory. Christianity is a practical religion. When you repent, something definite will happen to you, something of which you and others will be aware. Your sins, which in the Scriptures are pictured as a great burden, will be lifted up and removed from you, and you will be free in Christ.

Repentance, then, brings complete transformation; and it is our desire for this transformation which leads us to repent. During the days of Evangelist Billy Sunday, a notoriously evil man was converted. He repented and his sins were remitted. His wife, however, instead of being glad at her husband's conversion, was angry because, as she said, she had no use for "religious fanatics." She filed suit for divorce, accusing him of almost every crime except murder. Believing that it was not God's will for him to oppose the divorce, he so stated to the court clerk, saying of the bill against him, "It is all true and more. But," he went on, "that man is dead." "Aren't you X.Y.?" asked the clerk in surprise, giving the name mentioned in the bill. "No," was the reply, "I'm a new man in Christ Jesus. X.Y. is dead. I'm only twenty-seven months old. The things named in that bill are blotted out by the blood of the Lamb. They are not on the books at all—only on your books." And he was right, for that is what happens to a person who repents. He becomes a new person. His past is blotted out. He is dead to it. He lives a new life, a life of forgiveness and joy.

What does remission of sins mean? The Greek word *aphesin,* translated "remission," comes from the preposition *apo,* meaning "from," and the verb *hieemi,* meaning "to send, to throw." Remission, then, is the throwing or sending away of something. Remission of sins is the sending or throwing away of our sins. The moment we repent, a mighty hand reaches down, picks up our sins, and casts them away from us. We do not get rid of them ourselves, but they are thrown away by the Lord Jesus Christ. What happened on the cross, therefore, when Jesus Christ took upon Himself our sins, becomes our conscious experience when we repent. Our sins are transferred to Him. The Apostle Peter vividly expresses this transaction when he says, "Who his own self bare our sins in his own body on the tree, that we, being dead to sins, should live unto righteousness: by whose stripes ye were healed" (I Peter

2:24). This we must understand clearly, that no man can remit sins, because the Lord Jesus Christ, whose exclusive purpose in coming into this world was to bear our sins on the cross, was the One who died for our sins, and no one else. He paid the penalty of our sin with His own blood and therefore He is the only One who can forgive or remit sins. We must understand beyond the shadow of a doubt that salvation is not a do-it-yourself project or one in which you can let others help you. It is the result of utter and complete dependence on Christ to reach down and lift our sins from us and free us from the penalty of sin, since He has paid it Himself.

But doesn't John 20:23 state that the disciples of Christ in New Testament times, and by implication priests and ministers today, can forgive sins? Doesn't it say, "Whose soever sins ye retain, they are retained"? If this verse were to be correctly and literally translated from the Greek, it would read like this: "If of any ones ye dismiss the sins, they have been dismissed; if of any ye retain, they have been retained." In other words, you declare the sins removed because they have already been removed by God Himself, or you declare them retained because the individual has not exercised faith in Jesus Christ, who consequently has not stooped down to remove them. (See the detailed exegesis of this verse in the author's book, *The Behavior of Belief*, section 3, pp. 182-5.)

Remission involves two things. The first is release from captivity. Prior to repentance and the consequent remission of sin, man is the slave of sin. The only way he can be free from the bondage of sin is to repent. A converted Hindu who presented himself for baptism said that for years he had been searching for the way of happiness in holy places in the river and in other religious ceremonies, but all in vain. When he heard the Word of Christ, he could not rest. He sat up one whole night in great distress of mind over his sins. When asked how he lost them he said, "They went away in thinking of Christ." That thinking of Christ was repentance unto remission of sins. To be free of the fear and guilt of sin, we must repent and obtain remission of sins.

The second thing that is involved in the remission of sins is pardon, cancellation of an obligation, a punishment, or guilt. There are some who take the part of confessors and when people come to them repenting of their sins, they impose upon them certain penances, in other words, man-imposed punishments. But this is totally contrary to the provisions of the Bible, for a person whose sins are remitted by Christ is free from the obligation of punishment. After all, how many times should sin be paid for? Has not Christ paid the penalty in full?

A minister once asked a group of children who were reading a version of the Bible that had translated the word *metanoia* as "penance" instead of "repentance" whether they could tell him the difference between the two words. A short silence followed and then a little girl asked, "Is it not this: Judas did penance, and went and hanged himself; Peter repented and wept bitterly?" It may be that Judas thought that by hanging himself he could blot out the guilt of sin. Instead he increased it. No infliction of punishment, either self-imposed or ordered by a clergyman, can result in the removal of our guilt of sin. The sending away of our sins can only be achieved by Christ Himself as we repent of our sins and trust Him. In repentance there must be an element of belief, of faith, as we shall see in our next study. We cannot work out our own pardon through what we do, but we can obtain our pardon through believing in Christ and what He did for us.

It is interesting to note that the word "sin" here is in the plural and appears without the definite article. The plural form, we believe, indicates that there is no sin which cannot be removed when we repent. The blood of the Lord Jesus Christ can cleanse us from all sin, every individual sin and all of them put together.

And it is not only man's original sin (that which constitutes us sinful) which can be remitted when we repent for the first time, but also all consequent sins. The continuity and constancy of repentance involved in the use of the present imperative form of "repent," *metanoiete,* applies also to the remission of our sins. Once we repent and are born again, we become new creatures in Christ Jesus. But unfortunately we do fall into sin, if only into the sin of falling short of the highest possible mark set in the Word of God. Nevertheless, it is still sin, even if it is merely in the realm of disposition. For even these sins of the refined spiritual life there is remission through repentance.

The fact that there is no definite article in front of the word *hamartioon,* "sins," would lead us to conclude that the underlying thought here is that no reference is made to specific sins. Sometimes it is possible to have committed sins and yet to be ignorant of them. This is why there is real value in the prayer that always ends with a request to God to forgive our sins. He is always willing to do it, if we are willing to confess that we must have committed some, since we are not perfect.

CAN YOU HAVE REPENTANCE WITHOUT FAITH OR FAITH WITHOUT REPENTANCE?

In Mark 1:15 we find that, along with the commandment to repent, the Lord Jesus Christ gave a joint commandment to believe. He said, "Repent ye, and believe the gospel." Why did the Lord put repentance before faith? And why did Matthew leave out the commandment to believe? Why command us first to repent and then to believe?

As we read the New Testament, we see that the two terms—repentance and belief—are inseparable. It is because in all genuine repentance there is belief, and in belief there is genuine repentance, that we sometimes find both terms used and sometimes only one. But whenever the one is used, the other is understood as a necessary corollary. It is the same as if we said that the periphery of a triangle is a certain length or gave the length of each side separately. There are certain Biblical terms that are inclusive of their prerequisites. On the other hand, when a distinction is desired in the specific significance and value of each, they are given separately, as the three sides of a triangle might be given instead of its total periphery. So it is in the case of repentance, belief, remission of sins, and even baptism. When forgiveness of sins is mentioned, we must always presuppose that it is based on repentance and belief. It makes no difference whether remission of sins is mentioned alone or in conjunction with repentance only, or faith only, or both. The same holds true of baptism.

There are some who have misunderstood some expressions using the term "baptism" when referring to water baptism. They have taken it to mean merely the ordinance of water baptism instead of everything that leads to water baptism. For a person to reach the place where he voluntarily asks to be baptized in water, he must have repented, believed in the Gospel, and had his sins forgiven by God through Christ. Otherwise, water baptism has no significance at all. Remember, then, as you encounter these terms that they must be interpreted in the general context of the Scriptures, not always taken to mean one isolated thing—although this is sometimes the case. When you ask for water to drink, you do not refuse it because it was brought to you in a glass, although you did not specifically ask for a "glass of water." Even so, when I say, "I have been baptized," I mean I have repented and believed in Christ and have had my sins forgiven. If baptism is not preceded by all these experiences, it is not the baptism of the New Testament; it is an empty word.

Belief, then, in the Gospel is the third great doctrine that was promulgated by our Saviour as He gave His first commandment. Mark makes sure to add that the message of the Lord Jesus was not only to repent, independently thought of, but also to believe in the Gospel. He wants us to realize that the only repentance that will result in remission of sins is the one accompanied by faith. We cannot stress repentance without bringing in faith, and we cannot stress faith without bringing in repentance. The two are inseparable and the time of their occurence is all but indistinguishable. Salvation is not all repentance, nor is it all faith. Repentance without the element of faith cannot save, and faith without repentance cannot save. Although repentance and faith are inseparable, they are distinct and particular in their meanings. Repentance does not mean faith, and vice versa. Let us not be confused on that point. But both are necessary if we are to receive the full benefits of the Gospel.

No doubt the Lord mentions repentance before He mentions belief in the Gospel, because He wants to acquaint us with the terms and conditions under which we can appropriate forgiveness. His forgiveness, which is inherent in the Gospel. At this point in His ministry He is just about to tell us what He is going to offer us in the Gospel—remission of sins. Only as we have our sins forgiven can we enter the Kingdom of Heaven. He wants to warn us to get ready. The means of appropriating forgiveness of sins is repentance, the stretching forth of our hands toward the offer to be made by God. It is significant that before God even makes this offer, He asks us to be ready to receive it, to accept it.

Is not this a further indication of the absolute confidence and trust man must exercise in the Words of Christ? Don't wait until you hear the specific offer, but stretch your hand out in expectation of its appearance. That is what the people in the Old Testament did. Christ had not come, but His coming was revealed in veiled form in the prophecies of His messengers. Those who repented as they looked toward the unseen and not yet incarnate Christ were undoubtedly saved and forgiven. Forgiveness to the people of the Old Testament did not come through the keeping of the Law of Moses—for no one ever kept it in its entirety—but through confidence in the Word of the coming Christ.

In the New Testament, in this new economy, we are saved through confidence, trust, faith in the Word of the Christ who has already come. "Repent," therefore, applies to all people—those who lived before Christ and those who came afterward. Before the invisible Christ becomes visible and faith becomes sight, we must repent. Where Christ is concerned, our confidence, so to speak, must be blind. When He says "Repent," we have to be prepared to stretch our hands of desperation toward Him, although we cannot see His hands stretched out to take hold of ours.

But it may be that the Lord was fearful that, if He mentioned repentance alone, we would incur the danger of thinking there is merit in our repentance, in our afterthoughts about sin, in our sorrow and tears over our sins, and in our determination to live differently. Nothing that we do ourselves can bring us remission of sins and salvation. Repentance is an act of will that we are called upon to perform; but without God's mighty hand to catch hold of ours and save us, such a step would be like moving into a vacuum. We must understand that what we do does not save us. It is merely a call upon Christ to save us. If he were not there to save us, all our crying and our repentance would be in vain. Our repentance is nothing if it is not based on the commandment of Christ and His explicit promise to save and forgive.

All this is expressed by the term "belief in the Gospel," which involves what God has done for us in Jesus Christ. The merit of our salvation, then, is not in what we do—repentance—but in what Christ did. We believe that is why Mark, whose Gospel was written first, adds to the commandment "Repent" the commandment to "Believe in the gospel." It may be that later on the meaning of the word "repent" was crystallized and carried inseparably along with it the element of belief in the Gospel, so that Matthew records Christ as simply saying "Repent."

Repentance of itself has no virtue that will cause Christ to forgive us. It is only the blood of Christ that can wash away the filth of our sinful natures. But the Lord wanted to let us know right from the very start that the blood of Christ will not have any effect upon us unless we do repent.

Repentance conceived of apart from the Gospel cannot bring about the forgiveness of sins. This is the kind of repentance Pharaoh manifested when he said, "I have sinned" (Exod. 9:27); or Balaam, who, in spite of saying "I have sinned" (Num. 22:34), never really experienced forgiveness; or Judas, who, after saying "I have sinned" (Matt. 27:4), went and hanged himself, which he would never have done had he experienced forgiveness.

The sinner who expects forgiveness of sins by virtue of the value of repentance has not genuinely repented and his act will not result in the desired forgiveness. We are not forgiven because we repent but because Jesus Christ died for our sins. The cause of our forgiveness is the sacrificial atonement of Jesus Christ. The means is our repentance. But the means can never take the place of the cause and would be entirely valueless without it. Repentance, then, as experienced by man, would be useless were it not for the blood of the Lord Jesus Christ, the merits of which are made available to man through belief in the Gospel. The Apostle Paul made this clear when he testified "both to the Jews, and also to the Greeks, repentance toward God, and faith toward our Lord Jesus Christ" (Acts 20:21). The two cannot be divorced. Repentance without faith is like reaching into a vacuum, and faith in the sacrifice of the Lord Jesus Christ without repentance is like believing in the existence of a life rope without ever trying to catch hold of it and secure your personal safety. The work of Christ needs to be appropriated, and this can only be done through that first step—repentance, deep sorrow for sin, and determination to throw oneself upon the mercy of Christ. We must clearly understand that Christ will not save us unless we repent, unless we ask Him to save us in contrition of heart and faith. On the other hand, if our repentance is not accompanied by faith in His sufficiency to save us, it is worthless.

DOES A MORAL PERSON NEED TO REPENT?

It is harder to persuade a moral person of his need of repentance than anyone else. "I am a good man," he will object indignantly. "I am a moral person. Of what shall I repent?" Morality can be a very dangerous thing when it is thought of as taking the place of what Christ came to do for man. If morality were sufficient to assure a man's salvation, why was it necessary for Christ to die on the cross? Again our moralist says, "Well, He died for sinners, not for moral men like me." And so, comforting himself with his morality and blinded by self-righteousness, he deprives himself of the very heaven he feels so sure he deserves. You may feel particularly pleased with yourself, your character, and your works, but are you sure God sees you in the same light?

Moody used to say, "You can always tell when a man is a great way from God—he is always talking about himself, how good he is. But the moment he sees God by the eye of faith, he is down on his knees, and, like Job, he cries, 'Behold, I am vile.' " This is not an easy realization to come to—to see that while you may be morally clean you are vile in your own self-righteousness.

The other day my little boy came to me from school with the evidence of what he had had for lunch smeared all over his mouth. I told him to go wash his face and come back to show me the results. He returned in a hurry, saying, "I'm all clean now, Daddy." "Are you?" I asked. "Sure. I washed just like you told me to." From his point of view he was clean, but from where I stood he still looked dirty. It is not what we think of ourselves that counts, but what God our Creator thinks of us. We may seem moral to ourselves, and meet all human standards of morality, but will this suffice for entrance into the Kingdom of God? The kings and rulers of this earth set their own standards for admittance to their domains; but since it is the Kingdom of God we are talking about, we must permit Him to set the rules of admittance.

It is evident from an examination of the New Testament that repentance that is based merely on the moral law is not sufficient. Though the moral law is the natural consequence of the Gospel, it does not itself include the Gospel. This is aptly illustrated by the story of the rich young ruler in Luke 18:18-25. When this young man came to Jesus, he said, "Good Master, what shall I do to inherit eternal life?" The Lord Jesus directed him to keep the commandments, the moral law of God, with which he was already acquainted. But he was a moral young man who said that he had kept all these commandments from his youth up, and the Lord did not try to refute him. He sought to show him that, in spite of being moral, he needed something else to enable him to acquire eternal life, the life of God, which is a life of forgiveness and holiness. All he had done was good, but it was not enough. The Lord told him that he still lacked one thing. It was the absence of that that had prompted him to come to the Saviour in the first place. He was moral and yet a sinner.

Now many people are under a misapprehension concerning the command which the Lord gave this young man. He told him, "Yet lackest thou one thing: sell all that thou hast, and distribute unto the poor, and thou shalt have treasure in heaven: and come, and follow me." What was it that the young man objected to and did not accept? We believe that fundamentally it was not the selling of his goods, but the command, "Come, and follow me." This involved believing on the Lord Jesus Christ. The young ruler could not follow Christ if he did not believe on Him; but once he believed on Him there was nothing that he would not be willing to do for Him, not only to give up his riches but his very life for His sake.

Here is a man who was moral and yet a sinner. He felt the need of forgiveness but wanted to earn it by his own works, instead of accepting what Christ had done and was going to do. No matter how much of the law man is able to keep, there is always something lacking. That is belief in Christ. It is his sinful nature that needs to be dealt with, and he cannot do this himself. That is Christ's work. No man can die for his own sins and then go on to lead a life pleasing to God. But because Christ died for our sins, we can live by appropriating His sacrifice. This requires humility—the willingness to admit our imperfections and to concede that God can do something for us that we cannot do for ourselves.

Another illustration of this truth—that mere repentance and a devout, moral life are not enough for the remission of sins—is the story of Cornelius. Acts 10:2 tells us that he was a devout man, and one that feared God with all his house, which gave much alms to the people, and prayed to God alway." This could not be said of many people. His good reputation was undisputed among his contemporaries and confirmed by the Scriptures. Yet it is apparent that, like the young ruler, he felt a lack in his life. We are told that his prayers were heard, and that his alms were had in remembrance before God. And yet an angel appeared to tell him to send to Joppa for Peter the Apostle, who would tell him what to do (Acts 10:32). "But what else is there to do?" you ask. The man was devout; he feared God, was a true philanthropist, prayed to God always, and his prayers were heard and his alms remembered by God. Does a person who does all these things need anything more? Can he not be counted as a believer, one whose sins are forgiven?

Now observe what Peter told him: "To him [the

Lord Jesus Christ] give all the prophets witness, that through his name whosoever believeth in him shall receive remission of sins" (Acts 10:43). This clearly indicates that in spite of Cornelius' repentance, good works, and earnest devotion, his sins were not forgiven. Probably he did all these things in order to commend himself to God and obtain remission of sins, instead of his good works being the outcome of his divine forgiveness. But in order to obtain forgiveness of sins he needed to believe on the Lord Jesus Christ.

God is not deaf to the cry of a yearning heart such as Cornelius'. His morality and good works went up as a memorial, but they did not produce forgiveness of his sins. The Lord, looking upon the earnestness of his soul, directed Peter to show him the only way by which his prayers and gifts could be not merely remembered but accepted by the Lord of Heaven. There is a difference between remembrance and acceptance. Our good works are accepted by the Lord when they are the result of our faith in Christ, but they are merely remembered when they come from an unforgiven heart. Cornelius was sincere but he was not perfect. God will not accept anything that is imperfect. And only the Lord Jesus Christ has that perfection which is acceptable in God's sight. Therefore, by receiving Christ, we have His righteousness imputed to us and become perfect in the sight of God. What we are—forgiven sinners—and what we have, then ascend to God, not merely as memorable, but as acceptable to Him.

Repentance of itself, even though it may include sincere obedience to the moral law of God, will not bring about forgiveness of sins or reconciliation with God. This can take place only through faith in the work of Christ, through His shed blood on the cross of Calvary. Therefore repentance which is not accompanied by belief in Jesus Christ is not genuine,

New Testament repentance. In this connection we should observe that baptism with water always followed the exercise of faith, and did not substitute for it.

From what we have said, we can see why this commandment of Christ to repent and believe in the Gospel is addressed not only to out-and-out sinners but also to those who consider themselves righteous and who are considered devout by others. To the moral and immoral, to the humanly righteous and the unrighteous, to all, the Lord Jesus commands, "Repent ye, and believe the gospel."

THE SIAMESE TWINS OF THE GOSPEL

The New Testament contains two distinct doctrines which may be said to be like Siamese twins. We cannot separate them, and yet they have two distinct personalities. Each is indispensable to the other, however, if either is to have life. These two doctrines are repentance and faith. Without repentance we cannot go to Christ, and without faith we cannot receive what Christ offers—the forgiveness of sins. Without repentance, faith is a groundless presumption; and without faith, repentance is a mere hypocritical expression of intention.

These two terms, repentance and faith (or belief), are so inseparable in the New Testament and in the whole Bible that each is used many times to include the other. The end result of both is the remission of sins, or salvation. We need not be surprised, therefore, when only one—either repentance or belief—is mentioned as capable of procuring this end result. Faith is incorporated in repentance, and repentance includes faith.

For instance, when Peter preaches to the Jews (Acts 3:19), inviting them to repent, he says, "Repent ye therefore, and be converted, that your sins may be blotted out." But here repentance includes faith in the Lord Jesus Christ. Peter had just been speaking of Christ and His work of redemption. By inviting the Jews to repent, he was indicating to them the method of appropriating the work of Christ.

When the Philippian jailer asked Paul and Silas, "What must I do to be saved?" they replied, "Believe on the Lord Jesus Christ, and thou shalt be saved, and thy house" (Acts 16:30, 31). Was Paul contradicting Peter? Peter preached repentance and Paul preached faith, but no contradiction is involved. The one who preached repentance meant faith to be included in it, and the one who preached faith meant repentance along with it. The Lord Jesus made it absolutely clear in His preaching that we must not only repent but also believe the Gospel (Mark 1:15).

Now what does it mean to believe the Gospel? We hear the phrase often, but have we ever stopped to analyze it?

What is the Gospel? The word in the original Greek text is *euangelion,* made up of the adverb *eu,* meaning "good, well, happy, joyous, glad," and the word *angelion,* which comes from the verb root *angelloo,* meaning "to announce." "Gospel," therefore, means good announcement, good news, a good, joyful, glad message. In English the word has exactly the same etymological derivation. In the ancient Saxon language, the word "God" signifies a word or message. The word originally was "Godspell," which meant God's Word and also a good message, or glad tidings, or good news. Thus no better word could be found in English to translate the Greek word *euangelion.* It is God's good, joyful message.

In the Old Testament, whenever the prophets referred to the coming of Christ, they spoke of Him as bringing a joyful and happy message to the world. Isaiah says, "How beautiful upon the mountains are the feet of him that bringeth good tidings, that publisheth peace; that bringeth good tidings of good, that publisheth salvation" (Isa. 52:7). And in the prophecy of Nahum we read, "Behold upon the mountains the feet of him that bringeth good tidings" (1:15). There is no doubt that it was the coming of Christ that these prophets had in mind: for when the Lord Jesus was born, the angel who was sent to tell the shepherds of the event announced it thus: "Behold, I bring you good tidings [*euangelizomai,* the same word in its verbal form] of great joy, which shall be to all people" (Luke 2:10). The meaning of the coming of Christ into the world was made fully manifest through the heavenly song, "Glory to God in the highest, and on earth peace, good will toward men" (Luke 2:14).

The word *euangelion* is characteristically a New Testament word, and constitutes the heart of the New Testament message. That is why the historical record of the coming, life, work, death, and resurrection of the Lord Jesus Christ is called the "Gospel" of Matthew, the "Gospel" of Mark, the "Gospel" of Luke, and the "Gospel" of John. These books contain the joyful news of God's message of good will toward men: that they will not be punished for their sins, because Christ, the Son of God, is to die for them; and whoever believes on Him will be freed from sin, will be forgiven.

In Classical Greek, the word *euangelion* had three meanings. Originally it stood for the reward given to a messenger for bringing good tidings. It is with this meaning that it is used in the Septuagint, in II Samuel 4:10. Later it came to mean the sacrifices made to the gods when such good tidings were received. And finally, in Hellenistic Greek, it came to mean the good tidings themselves. In the Septuagint, it is used for the good tidings of victory (I Sam. 31:9), the good tidings of the birth of a child (Jer. 20:15); and occasionally it was used to indicate tidings of any kind.

In the Old Testament, men sometimes seemed to have an unhealthy fear of God, whom they imagined to be cruel and revengeful. God's revelation produced terror instead of joy. This arose out of an inability to comprehend God's actions and purposes. God's purposes are eternal and unchanging. They were no different in the Old Testament from what they are in the New. His purposes and declarations were merely veiled in prophetic language in the Old

Testament, whereas in the New the veil was torn and the revelation became full and clear. Thus it cannot be said that the Gospel appeared for the first time with the birth of Christ. The Gospel was proclaimed for the first time in Genesis 3:15, when God said to the serpent which was representative of Satan and responsible for the fall of man, "I will put enmity between thee and the woman, and between thy seed and her seed; it shall bruise thy head, and thou shalt bruise his heel." The seed of the woman was to be the Lord Jesus Christ. And even at this early stage, the Virgin Birth was predicted. The Lord Jesus was born of the seed of a woman and not of a man and woman, as is ordinarily the case. Yes, Satan would bring great calamities upon man, but finally in Christ he would receive his death blow. This is the first proclamation of the good news of Satan's defeat and the redemption of man.

Some people try to make a distinction between the Gospel of God and the Gospel of Christ. Surely this is erroneous; for the Gospel is sometimes designated as "the gospel of God." In Mark 1:14 we read, "Now after that John was put in prison, Jesus came unto Galilee, preaching the gospel of the kingdom of God." The best manuscripts omit the words "of the kingdom" and simply say "preaching the gospel of God." And as Paul writes to the Thessalonians he says, "We were bold in our God to speak unto the gospel of God with much contention" (I Thess. 2:2). He also refers to the Gospel as "the gospel of God" in verses 8 and 9. The good news of God was the same good news of Christ. We do not have one God of the Old Testament and another of the New. In God there is no variableness or shadow of turning. It is a mistake to speak of a God of terror and wrath and a Christ of love. The Lord Jesus simply revealed the full nature of God, that He is indeed love; that He so loved us that He sent His Son to die for us, that whosoever believes on Him will have eternal life. This is the Gospel of God and the Gospel of Christ, the only Gospel ever preached to the world, made possible through the sacrifice of the Lord Jesus Christ. Those who lived before the incarnation of God in Christ looked forward to it as prophesied, and those of us who live after the incarnation look back. Anyone who refuses, therefore, to believe in the Gospel and to accept this wonderful news that Jesus Christ paid the penalty of our sins so that we might have full and free forgiveness, is inexcusable.

WHAT IS BELIEF IN THE GOSPEL?

The coming of Christ into this world, His life, His work, His death, and His resurrection are God's good news to man. They are the Gospel. Why are they called good news? An understanding of this will help us to realize why it is important for us to accept it. Not to listen and believe it is folly.

When the Lord Jesus Christ addressed Himself to all people in commanding them to repent and believe the Gospel, He indicated that all were in need of repentance and faith. But since only sinners need to repent and believe, we must conclude that, in the judgment of the Lord Jesus Christ, everyone is a sinner, no matter what he thinks of himself. This is corroborated by the Apostle Paul, who says that the law made "all the world . . . guilty before God" (Rom. 3:19); and that "All have sinned and come short of the glory of God" (Rom. 3:23). This is an inescapable indictment, as further attested to in Romans 5:12: "Wherefore, as by one man sin entered into the world, and death by sin; and so death passed upon all men, for that all have sinned." This clearly indicates that the entire posterity of Adam is under sin and therefore under the penalty of sin, which is eternal death, separation from God the Creator (see Romans 6:23). Naturally, then, we are all spiritually dead, separated from God. This could hardly be considered as the Gospel, or good news. It was bad news brought about by man's disobedience.

God ordained the shedding of innocent blood as the means for cleansing from sin. "Without shedding of blood is no remission" (Heb. 9:22). Logically, each one of us should have to die for his own sin, and even then we could not procure forgiveness. But instead of exacting the death penalty from us, God in the person of Jesus Christ became man—without sin—and suffered in our stead. This is the wonderful news of the Gospel. Christ died for us and in our stead to satisfy the justice of the Father. When we accept what He has done for us, we are free from the penalty of our sin and therefore can have the assurance that our sins are forgiven or remitted. This is the only way we can receive remission of sins. Christ "was delivered for our offences and was raised again for our justification" (Rom. 4:25). He "gave himself a ransom for all, to be testified in due time" (I Tim. 2:6). And as Paul says in Ephesians 5:2, "Christ also hath loved us, and hath given himself for us an offering [for sin] and a sacrifice to God for a sweet-smelling savour." Previously he had told us, "It is in his blood that we have redemption, even the remission of sins" (literal translation of Eph. 1:7). These declarations of the Word of God make it clear that the Lord Jesus Christ, in becoming man and going to Calvary, took upon Himself the punishment that belonged to us for our sins against God. Isn't this good news? Could there be any better?

The big question is how the individual may secure the benefits of what Christ did for all men. Since we are adjured to exercise individual belief throughout the Scriptures, we must conclude that the death of Christ is valueless to those who do not personally appropriate it by faith. In other words, Christ's death did not automatically confer redemption upon the entire world. Redemption is like air: it is free for all to breathe, but only those who do breathe it benefit from it.

What, then, does it mean to believe in the Gospel? It means to take advantage of it. In John 3:18 we read, "He that believeth on him [Christ] is not condemned: but he that believeth not is condemned already." Each individual is responsible for his own condemnation or release from the guilt and penalty of sin. Now in what respect does repentance differ from faith in procuring our salvation? Repentance qualifies us for pardon and salvation, but it cannot purchase it or obtain it for us.

As Bishop Beveridge says, "There is no such virtue in the tears of repentance as to wash away the guilt of sin; neither can the fig-leaves of our own righteousness hide our nakedness from the eyes of an all-seeing God. Moses may and should lead us through the wilderness; but it is only Joshua, or Jesus, can carry us into Canaan. The moral law must direct our steps; but it is the Gospel only that can save our souls. So that if we ever desire to sail into the haven of eternal happiness, it must be through the blood of Christ, by whom alone it is that our former sins can be pardoned, our present lusts subdued, our persons justified before God here, and our souls glorified with him hereafter. And it is only by Christ we can be saved, so we cannot be saved by him without faith. Nothing that we do will please God; and without faith, nothing that Christ hath done will profit us; his wounds will not heal us, nor his blood cleanse us; his merit will not be imputed to us, nor his Spirit implanted in us, unless we believe in Him." (*The Works of the Right Rev. William Beveridge,* Vol. V, p. 11.)

But though all this may be thoroughly understood by those of us who have believed in Christ, it is often strange and incomprehensible to those who have not. When we invite people to believe in the Gospel, we must explain to them what it really means. Understanding is a prerequisite to effective doing. In such an important matter, upon which our eternal destiny hinges, we must thoroughly understand the beliefs upon which we are called to act.

Faith, or the act of believing, cannot be performed through any bodily activity, but like repentance must be an act of the mind and heart. The assent of the mind and will to what is declared by another person is faith, is believing. Of course, this involves confidence in the authority of the person who makes the declaration. Our acceptance as true of what someone else tells us will depend a great deal on our estimate of the trustworthiness of that person, as well as on an examination of what he actually says. Believing someone, then, is accepting what he says and what he is.

No exercise of faith is involved, however, if what is said is subject to examination and verification by the senses. Many things are credible because they are apparent to our senses, and our accepting them, therefore, even when others tell us about them, is not believing in the sense of the word as used in the Scriptures. If someone tells us that the whole is greater than any of its parts, we can readily see and test this for ourselves. Taking his word for it is not really an exercise of faith. The fact is apparent and easily proved.

This is the fundamental difference between natural science and faith. Natural science does not call for belief, because it deals with the material realm, which is subject to the laws of evidence and rationalization. But faith depends on the unsupported testimony of another and therefore rests on the authority of the one making the affirmation, without the facts being apparent in themselves, either to sense or reason.

This is an age when business could not possibly move ahead without the credit system. What is meant by saying a man has good credit? He can go into a store and buy a great many things without paying for them. His name, his character, his word are the things trusted and acted upon. In like manner in the spiritual realm, we believe everything which Christ has declared. We cannot prove the veracity of His words either by the test tube or by our reason, either by natural experiment or logic. But we can still believe them absolutely because of the One who spoke them, who declared Himself to be Truth and proved it by His birth, His life, His death, His resurrection, and His ascension. Present me with another such person and I will believe everything He says. The credit of the Lord Jesus Christ is good.

Would any reputable scientist today have the temerity to deny the reality of the unseen and invisible? A smart assistant professor once said to his students, "If you have science and faith in your mind, you had better keep them in watertight compartments, for if by any chance they should intermingle, faith would disappear in the precipitation that would take place." Contrast this with what Pasteur, the great French scientist, said: "It is not a question of faith and science, but it is a question of the size of the mind. If you have only a little bucket of a mind and get a lot of science into it, the little faith that you may have may come up floating out at the top and be lost; but if you have a good sized bucket of a mind there will be plenty of room for both science and faith."

Let's stretch our minds to "big-bucket" size, to accept both science and faith—both the visible and the invisible—as real. Some of the visible we can discover and verify, but the invisible we must accept or reject on the authority of the one who reveals it. The One who has revealed the invisible things of God to us is the Lord Jesus Christ. We have historical evidences of what He was, what He did, how He died, and how He rose from the dead. He came to earth to be seen, to establish His divine authority, and thus to make what He had to say about the invisible realities of the universe believable and trustworthy. If we are to know the truth, we must not close our eyes to Christ, the historical Person, for in Him we shall find the only One whom we can believe when He tells us the otherwise unbelievable. Many have made wild claims, but not one has risen from the dead as Christ did. Faith means believing what He tells us about what we cannot see or verify through the other senses.

We can receive nothing from Christ unless we exercise faith in Him and what He says. He will not be able to forgive us our sins unless we believe that He is the only One qualified to do so. Repentance is a humbling of ourselves; it is like taking the lid off our hearts so that the grace of God may fill us. Faith is our invitation to Christ to fill us with His grace. The result is forgiveness of sins and reconciliation with God. God then becomes our Father, for we have confidence in Him.

A Christian worker was trying to lead a young man to accept the grace of God in Christ by faith alone. The young man suddenly turned upon him and said, "I will never believe until I have an experience." The Christian worker flashed back, "You will never have an experience until you believe." And that is absolutely true. You can never experience the forgiveness of sins unless you believe in the Gospel, and believing in the Gospel involves first believing in the One who made the Gospel possible and declared it to us, the Lord Jesus Christ. His credit is good. Take Him at His Word. His testimony alone is infallible. He proved it by His death and resurrection. No one else ever made the assertion, "He that cometh to me shall never hunger; and he that believeth on me shall never thirst" (John 6:35). Reject the Gospel and the responsibility rests entirely upon you. Believe Christ and you will be amazed at the miracles that will follow.

WHY BELIEVE IN THE GOSPEL?

When Christ gave His first commandment, He called upon men not merely to repent but to believe in the Gospel.

It is interesting to note that not only the verb "repent," *metanoeite,* is in the present imperative (thus indicating a continuous and unceasing need for repentance after our initial sorrow for our sinful state), but also the verb "believe," *pisteute.* This means that once we begin to believe we continue to do so. The life of the Christian is a life of continuous faith and trust. We do not become Christians by virtue of a single act of belief which ceases after it has received what it was after. In other words, we do not come to the Lord Jesus Christ at a particular time in our lives to accept Him as Saviour and then go forth on our own. This is not the idea of belief as set forth in the Scriptures. We are told to keep on believing.

A child receives life from his mother, but when he enters into the world he also receives it as a result of taking his first breath, and from then on he must continue to breathe if he is to live. The first drawing in of breath insures the rest, and his continuous breathing is proof that there was an initial intake of breath. In like manner, we receive our life from God, but we also begin the Christian life as the result of an act of faith. This is the first breath, so to speak. If we were to translate this twin commandment of Christ's literally, we would say, "Keep on repenting and keep on believing in the Gospel," or paraphrased more fully, "Repent once and continue to repent; and believe once and continue to believe in the Gospel." Our spiritual life can never exist apart from its source. Since it comes from the life of God within us, we must never delude ourselves with the notion that we can break our communion and relationship with the Giver of life and live. The continuation of breathing after that first breath of faith is natural. It will involve no special effort. A live person lives. A believer believes every moment of his spiritual life.

In the best manuscripts, this expression is given as "believe in the gospel" (*pisteuete en too euangelioo*) instead of "believe the gospel." Many attempts have been made to explain why the proposition "in" is used instead of the verb taking a direct object. Peculiarly, this is the only place in Scripture where this proposition is used with the verb *pisteuoo*, "believe." Deissman, who has studied the question carefully, believes that this preposition is meant to designate the sphere of the Gospel. In this light, we would venture the following exegesis:

When a person repents and believes the Gospel for the first time, he moves from the sphere of Adam to the sphere of Christ. (See author's article on I Corinthians 15:22, in *Moody Monthly*, April, 1960.) Once man has entered that sphere, he cannot live as an independent entity. He has to exercise full reliance upon Christ, without whom there would be no good news or Gospel. This definitely destroys the theory that one need only be concerned with making a public confession of accepting Christ or the Gospel and then feel free to live outside the sphere of the Gospel. Once a person has repented and entered this circle of those whom Christ has redeemed, he is under obligation to keep on believing. It takes just as much faith to live within the sphere of the Gospel as it does to leave the sphere of Adam and enter the sphere of Christ in the first place. The Christian's new birth is the result of faith, but the Christian life is also the result of constant and uninterrupted faith in the Gospel.

This indicates to us that the Christian life is made up of constant conscious experiences of repenting and believing. The Christian, if he is honest with himself and God, will confess that although he is in the sphere of the Gospel, or Christ, that sphere is still in the world; and as long as it—and we—are in the world, we shall be surrounded by sin, temptation, and the possibility of yielding. Otherwise there would be no need of constant repentance and belief. Belief within this circle of Christ involves the realization of our constant dependence upon Him.

The commandment of Christ in Mark 1:15 says, "Believe in the gospel," and not "believe in Christ." The implication is that in the circle of believers there is constant need for the practice of God's good news toward men. The Lord is ready to forgive us, at all times, even within the sphere of our Christian experience, if we will only repent and believe. He will also graciously forgive those who are still outside the sphere of the Gospel so that they may enter the sphere of Christ. For the unregenerate, forgiveness involves entrance; for the Christian, it involves maintenance of holiness within. The first involves the birth of a spiritual life, and the second involves the growth of that life and its upkeep. Both are important, and in giving us this command to keep on believing in the Gospel the Lord shows us that He is concerned about both.

The Scriptures give two reasons why the Lord urges repentance and belief upon every man. Matthew mentions only one: "Repent: for the kingdom of heaven is at hand" (4:17); while Mark records the Lord as saying, "The time is fulfilled, and the kingdom of God is at hand: repent ye, and believe the gospel" (1:15).

We shall take as the first reason the one mentioned by both evangelists: "The kingdom of heaven [or the kingdom of God] is at hand." Some Bible teachers seek to make a distinction between the Kingdom of Heaven and the Kingdom of God. The two expressions are nearly equivalent, although

Matthew is the only one who speaks of the Kingdom of Heaven. It does not occur elsewhere in the New Testament. Only in II Timothy 4:18 do we find a similar expression, "his heavenly kingdom." The expression "kingdom of God," on the other hand, occurs only four times in Matthew (6:33, 12:28, 21:31, 43), but it occurs often in Mark and Luke and occasionally in the other books of the New Testament. Other references in the New Testament are to the kingdom of the Father (Matt. 26:29, Mark 11:10), the kingdom of the Son (Luke 22:30), of the Son of man (Matt. 13:41), etc. The Kingdom is thus one in its basic meaning. It is the Kingdom of God, and that Kingdom, since it is of God, is heavenly—the Kingdom of Heaven. In order not to become confused, we must remember that these terms sometime refer to the Kingdom of God (or Heaven) which is present in a spiritual sense, and sometime to the earthly physical presence of the King upon this earth. The context determines which meaning is intended.

A kingdom is an area over which someone exerts absolute influence and control. At the present time, where is the Kingdom of God to be found? Only in mysterious form (Mark 4:11) in the hearts of believers—those who have repented and believed in the Gospel. When a person is born again, the Kingdom of God is said to enter within him. Here the term is synonymous with Christ, the King. When we receive Christ into our hearts and lives, we also receive and acknowledge His absolute rule. He is our King. His Kingdom is within us.

Once the Pharisees asked the Lord Jesus when the Kingdom of God should come, thinking of it as some temporal, physical kingdom to be established on earth. They wanted Christ—if He really was King of the Jews—to go ahead and establish His kingdom so that everyone might see it. But the Lord said,

"Neither shall they say, Lo here! or, lo there! for, behold, the kingdom of God is within you" (Luke 17:21). Of course, the Kingdom of God was not within the unbelieving Pharisees, but within those who truly believed; and it is not unlikely that the Lord pointed to His disciples as He spoke. For as the Lord made clear to Nicodemus, unless a man receives a spiritual rebirth—the new birth from on high—he cannot even see the Kingdom of God (John 3:5). Thus the Kingdom of God may be taken as synonymous with Christ entering into man's heart and life in a spiritual, mysterious way, and taking absolute possession and control.

The Kingdom of God is also indicated in the New Testament as the sphere of Christ in which Christ or God is the absolute Ruler of all within the circle of the redeemed, those who have repented and believed and thus entered the family of God. We are said to enter it in this manner when we accept or receive Christ. The Kingdom of God, in this respect, is the family of God on earth. "Verily I say unto you," declared the Lord Jesus, "Except ye be converted, and become as little children, ye shall not enter into the kingdom of heaven" (Matt. 18:3). To encourage those who are persecuted for righteousness' sake, our Lord assured them that "theirs is the kingdom of heaven" (Matt. 5:10). There is a family of God within the family of the world. And to enter this family of God—the smaller circle within the larger circle—one must be born again.

What did the Lord mean, then, when He said that we should repent and believe the Gospel because the Kingdom of God or Heaven is at hand? He was announcing that the King, Christ, who came to be the good news of salvation to everyone who repents and believes, is very close, waiting to enter every heart if that heart will humble itself in repentance and faith. This is the same thought as in Revelation 3:20, "Behold, I stand at the door and knock; if any man hear my voice, and open the door, I will come in to him, and will sup with him, and he with me." By declaring right from the beginning of His evangelistic mission that He was present to save, the Lord Jesus Christ was making it plain that there could be no human response if there were no divine initiative, if there were no Gospel.

The Lord Jesus gave two reasons why He invited men to repent and believe in the Gospel. One was that the Kingdom of God or Heaven was at hand. The other was that "the time is fulfilled."

In our last study we saw that the expression "Kingdom of Heaven, or God," is in this case equivalent to the King Himself, the Lord Jesus Christ who came to this earth to seek and to save that which was lost. When we allow the Kingdom of Heaven or God to come within us, we allow the King to reign in our lives. He becomes the Master.

The original Greek for the expression translated "is at hand," in Mark 1:15, is *eengiken,* which is the perfect indicative of the verb *engizoo,* meaning "to bring near" or "to come near." This is a verb of motion, which in the Septuagint is used transitively; that is, its action passes from the subject to the object. In the sentence, "I move a table near me," the verb is transitive. But in the New Testament the verb is always used intransitively. The subject acts upon itself. Here, where we are told that the Kingdom of God or Heaven is at hand—has approached, has come near—the idea is that it has come near by itself, of its own power and volition, independently of human influence. The Kingdom of God has come near, not because man deserved it, or exercised any influence to bring it about, but because of the sovereign and eternal will of God Almighty. This shows clearly that God's Kingdom has an objective reality apart from man. It exists without him before it finds entrance within him; and when it becomes a subjective reality for the believer, it still remains an objective reality for others who have not appropriated it. God is not only a mysterious personality within us, when we repent and believe, but He is also a mysterious and real personality outside of us. God is thus subjectively and objectively real. That is why we speak of Christ within the heart of the believer; yet when we pray to the Lord we pray not to One who is within, but to One who is an objective entity outside ourselves.

The Kingdom of Heaven or God, the Lord Jesus Christ, is very near each one of us. He came from heaven and from God, of His own will and power, to be near us but not in us. This is as far as He chose to go. He could have forced His way into all human hearts without asking their consent but that would have been just a mass process of superimposing His will, like rubber stamping every earthly human being with the words "Heaven" and "God." This would not be salvation but captivation; repentance would not be characterized by humility but by humiliation. No, God did not choose to make of us Christian automata, as some individuals and religious groups have done, seeking to reduce Christianity to a religion of the masses by mass baptisms. Since God did not choose to do this, what right has man to do so?

That is why both verbs used in the twin commandments of Christ, "repent" and "believe" (addressed primarily to the unconverted but to all people in general), require something of man. He is called upon to repent and to believe in the Gospel, although neither repentance nor faith in himself will earn him forgiveness. Only the blood of Christ can cleanse man from sin; but man is called upon to accept God's offer of forgiveness, and this acceptance is designated as repenting and believing. There is no merit in either faith or repentance, singly or combined. Forgiveness of sin is granted only and absolutely because of what Christ did and not because of what man does. But the appropriation of this forgiveness is man's responsibility. And that is why we preach the Gospel, to invite men and women to accept God's offer of salvation. Yet we must understand that no man by his refusal to repent and believe makes void the gift of God. God's Kingdom has come near, is near everyone, if he will only receive it through repentance and faith.

And now we come to the second reason why we are called upon to repent and believe in the Gospel. It is found in the expression, "The time is fulfilled," which occurs only in Mark 1:15. "The time is fulfilled, and the kingdom of God is at hand: repent ye, and believe [in] the gospel."

The word translated "time" here is *kairos* in Greek. There are two Greek words which indicate time, *kairos* and *chronos.* From the latter come many English words, such as chronology, chronometer, etc. Both Archbishop Trench in his *Synonyms of the New Testament,* and J. B. Lightfoot in his *Notes on the Epistles of St. Paul,* discuss the distinction between these two words. *Kairos* speaks of quality, and *chronos* speaks of quantity (Ammonius, p. 80). And as Lightfoot states, "In fact *chronos* denotes a period of time whether long or short, and hence in reference to any particular event 'the date.' *Kairos* on the other hand applies equally to place as to time (perhaps primarily to place rather than to time, as is generally the case), and signifies originally 'the fit measure' (compare the use of *kairos, e.g.* Aesch. Agam. 1343 *pepleegmai kairian pleegeen*). Hence in reference to time it is 'the right moment,' the opportunity for doing, or avoiding to do, anything, involving the idea of adaptation" (p. 70).

In Mark 1:15, then, *kairos* means the right time, the opportune time. It is as if the Lord were saying, This is the best time for you to repent and believe in the Gospel. This is your best opportunity. Today is the best day; now is the best moment for you to repent and believe.

If men could only understand what a valuable opportunity they have, when the Kingdom of God is so near them, to repent and believe. But unfortunately many trifle with their opportunities in the manner of children playing with sand. They fill their hands with the shining grains and then let them trickle through their fingers one by one, till they are all gone. Is that what you are doing with the opportunity you have at this very moment to repent and believe in the Gospel?

Long ago, in one of the old Greek cities, stood a remarkable statue. Every trace of it has vanished now; but we still have an epigram which gives us an excellent description of it and the lession which those wise old Greeks meant it to convey. The epigram is in the form of a conversation between a traveler and the statue:

"What is thy name, O statue?"
"I am called Opportunity."
"Who made thee?"
"Lysippus."
"Why are thou on thy toes?"
"To show how quickly I pass by."
"But why is thy hair so long on thy forehead?"
"That men may seize me when they meet me."
"Why, then, is thy head so bald behind?"
"To show that, when I have once passed, I cannot be caught."

Remember, Christ says, that the present opportunity may never be yours again. Seize it while it is near you.

What does the expression "is fulfilled" mean? In Greek it is *pepleerootai.* The Greek verb *pleeroo* is related to the substantive *pleerooma.* Lightfoot gives a detailed study of this basic word in his examination of the Epistle to the Colossians (*Saint Paul's Epistles to the Colossians and to Philemon,* pp. 257-273). He points out that one of the classical meanings of the word is "plentitude, fulness, totality, abundance." Couple this with the meaning of the word *kairos,* "time" or "opportunity," as explained above, and you will understand the beauty of the full meaning of the expression, "the time is fulfilled." The right moment, the most opportune time for you to repent and believe, is the present, which is yours in abundance; and therefore the presently available opportunity can also be said to be plentiful. In other words, man has never had a better opportunity to repent and believe than now, when the Lord Jesus Christ has come in person to the world. As Arndt and Gingrich say in their *Lexicon,* when the verb *pleero-oo* refers to time as here, it means "to fill up, to complete a period of time, for time to reach its end" (p. 677). To make this plain here is the object of this expression. Qualitatively, this is the best time. Your opportunity is full now, with the coming of God to this earth in the person of Jesus Christ.

This indicates, of course, that this is not the only opportunity man has had to repent and believe, but that this is the most abundant and opportune time. If this is so, then there must have been previous opportunities, through the preaching of the prophets, through many theophanies, and through the ministry of John the Baptist. No, the coming of Christ into the world did not present man with his first opportunity of repenting and believing. Didn't Isaiah say, "Let the wicked forsake his way, and the unrighteous man his thoughts: and let him return unto the Lord, and he will have mercy upon him; and to our God, for he will abundantly pardon" (Isa. 55:7)? And then Ezekiel cried, "Repent, and turn yourselves from all your transgressions; so iniquity shall not be your ruin" (Ezek. 18:30). Yes, man has had divine opportunities throughout the span of time to repent and believe; but never has the opportunity been so full and abundant and present as in the coming of the Son of God in person to this earth.

And the opportunity for repentance and belief is

complete with the coming of Christ. This is called the day of grace, the day of last opportunity. If you reject this opportunity, when God Himself has come to earth to ask you to repent and believe, there will be no hope for you.

An overladen coal barge stood in the river. A sailor reported to the captain that the water was gaining upon the vessel, but the captain drove him away with scoffing. Twice, thrice the warning was repeated, but each time it went unheeded. At last the barge began to give evidence of sinking. The captain ordered the men to the boats. As they took their places, he said, "See, I told you there was plenty of time." Then he took out his knife to cut the cable to the barge. He fell back with a cry of horror; the cable was an iron chain.

You say there is plenty of time to get into the lifeboat. But the longer you delay your repentance and belief the harder it will be to cut the chain and free yourself from the world and sin. "To day if ye will hear his voice, harden not your heart" (Psa. 95:7, 8). It is a solemn thing to say "tomorrow" when God says "today," for man's tomorrow and God's today may never meet. The word that comes from the eternal Christ is "now," and it is man's own choice that fixes his doom. "The time is fulfilled" means that this is the greatest and most fitting opportunity, but it is the last.

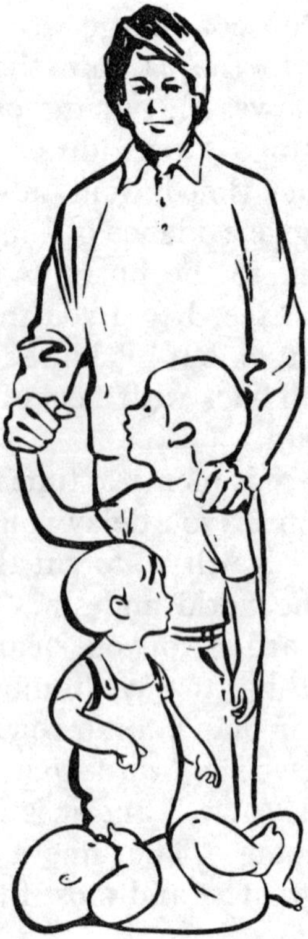

DOES CHRIST EXPECT US TO FOLLOW HIM BLINDLY?

After we have repented and believed in the Gospel, what is the next step? Is it enough simply to be a Christian, to have life from heaven, the life of God within us?

When we accept the Lord Jesus Christ as Saviour, a new life is born within us, the life of God. This is sometimes called eternal life, in contrast to our physical and psychic life as human beings, which is natural and temporal. When we repent and believe in the Lord Jesus Christ, we become something that we were not before. We acquire eternal life in addition to our temporal life.

In some ways this eternal life is analogous to physical life. When a child is born into the world, it is both perfect and imperfect. It is perfect in its make-up but imperfect in its development. Similarly, when we are born into the Kingdom of God, we are perfect in our spiritual make-up yet imperfect in growth and development. We have life, yet we do not really enjoy living except as we grow and become aware of all that can be ours in the spiritual life Christ gives.

It is this growth that we want to consider as we examine the further commandments of the Lord Jesus Christ. As we stated in our previous studies, only one commandment was given primarily to the unconverted and that was to repent and believe in the Gospel. We further indicated that this process of repentance is something that continues even after our initial entrance into the Kingdom of God. But there is more to the Christian life than repentance, something further than our initial step into the family of God. Surely, if you were invited to stay at a friend's house, you would not wish to remain in the foyer all the time but would like to enter further and enjoy every part of the house, including sitting at table and partaking of the delicious food prepared for you.

Thus, all the subsequent commandments of Christ that we shall examine have to do with the development of the Christian life. We shall consider them one by one, subjecting them to a careful examination, by the enablement of the Holy Spirit.

The second commandment of Christ is "Follow me." It is found in Matthew 4:19, which reads, "And he saith unto them, Follow me, and I will make you fishers of men." The same commandment is given in Mark 1:17 but with a slightly different wording. "And Jesus said unto them, Come ye after me, and I will make you to become fishers of men." In our study we shall seek to determine from the original Greek the reason for the variation in the wording of these two verses. What were the circumstances under which this commandment was given, and to whom was it addressed?

The commandment to follow Christ was given by our Lord Himself to Peter and Andrew, brothers. This was not on the occasion of their first meeting, however. He had already called them to repentance, and they had become His very own by believing the Gospel. How do we deduce this?

The first encounter that the Lord Jesus had with Simon Peter and Andrew is recorded in the Gospel of John. Andrew first heard the testimony of John the

Baptist about the Lord Jesus and followed Him. Later he brought his brother Simon Peter to Jesus (see John 1:35-42). And it was at this first encounter that the Lord changed the name of Simon to Cephas, or Peter.

The circumstance of this commandment in Matthew 4:19 and Mark 1:17 is not to be confused with the circumstances of Luke 5, where something similar occurred. In Luke 5:1 we find a great multitude pressing upon the Lord, whereas in Matthew 4:19 and Mark 1:17 He is alone. In Luke He is said to be standing, while in Matthew He is walking. In Luke the fishermen were washing their nets, having disembarked after their futile attempts to catch fish. In Matthew, Simon and Andrew are still in the boats casting their net. Thus we conclude that Matthew and Mark do not record the same incident as Luke.

The first thing we learn here is that, in order to follow the Lord Jesus, we must have Him within our heart. That was the case with Andrew and Peter, whom the Lord asked to follow Him. It is futile to try to follow someone we do not know and trust.

Men cannot become Christians by following Christ, but they follow Christ after they have become Christians. You follow Christ only if you have Him within your heart. The Greeks used to tell how Xenophon first met Socrates. It seems that they encountered each other in a narrow land, and Socrates barred the path with his stick. First Socrates asked Xenophon if he knew where he could buy this and that, and if he knew where this and that were made. Xenophon gave him the required information. Then Socrates asked him, "Do you know where men are made good and virtuous?" "No," replied the young Xenophon. "Then," said Socrates, "follow me and learn." It is true that one can learn by following; but one cannot follow Christ without first having experienced Christ. Many well-meaning people try to do what Christ did—such as loving their enemies—but they utterly fail. Why? Because it is not in human nature to love our enemies. We can only hate them. But if the Lord Jesus Christ indwells us, He loves our enemies through us, and we love our enemies through Him. Christ cannot be our Example unless He is first our Saviour. But it is essential that He become our Example after He has become our Saviour. The cart must move forward, but it can do so only as the horse is placed in its proper position—in front of it.

A poet and an artist each examined a painting by Poussin representing the healing of the two blind men of Jericho. The artist asked, "What seems to you the most remarkable thing in this painting?" The poet replied, "Everything in the painting is excellently given—the form of Christ, the grouping of the individuals, the expression in the faces of the leading characters—everything." The artist seemed to find the most significant touch elsewhere. Pointing to the steps of a house in the corner of the picture, he said, "Do you see that discarded cane lying there?" "Yes, but what does that signify?" "Why, my friend, on those steps the blind man sat with the cane in his hand but when he heard Christ come he was so sure that he would be healed that he let his cane lie there, since he would need it no more, and hastened to the Lord as if he could already see."

In asking us to follow Him, the Lord Jesus does not expect us to do it blindly. If we do not have the confidence which comes from faith in Him, any endeavor to follow Him will be a tortuous effort. But if we have received Him as Saviour and have experienced His healing touch upon us to deliver us from sin, then it will be our greatest pleasure to follow Him; it will seem the safest course in the world. But to see Christ in order to follow Him, we need His vision. No human eye can behold deity. We need

God to see God in Christ. How much more do we need God, through His Holy Spirit, to follow Him!

Dwight L. Moody gives us a fine illustration of the fact that the commandment of Christ to follow Him is given to His children and not to strangers. He says, "I was standing with a friend at his garden gate one evening when two little children came by. As they approached us, he said to me, 'Watch the difference in these two boys.' Taking one of them in his arms he stood him on the gatepost and, stepping back a few feet, he folded his arms and called to the little fellow to jump. In an instant the boy sprang toward him and was caught in his arms. Then turning to the second boy he tried the same experiment. But in the second case it was different. The child trembled and refused to move. My friend held out his arms and tried to induce the child to trust to his strength but nothing could move him. At last my friend had to lift him down from the post and let him go. 'What makes the difference in the two?' I asked. My friend smiled and said, 'The first is my own boy and knows me; but the other is a stranger's child whom I have never seen before.' And there was all the difference. My friend was equally able to prevent both from falling, but the difference was in the boys themselves. The first had assurance in his father's ability and acted upon it, while the second although he might have believed in the ability to save him from harm, would not put his faith into action."

Following Christ is impossible without being Christ's. If you try to follow Him without belonging to Him, you will always be in doubt about His motives and His treatment of you.

NO LOAFERS NEED APPLY

We have seen the commandment to follow Christ was given to the disciples who were already acquainted with Him and had no doubt already received Him as their Saviour and Lord. Now there is a second step that the Lord commands us to take if we are to experience all that is meant to be ours in our Christian walk.

The first encounter that the Lord Jesus had with Andrew was by the river Jordan, where John the Baptist was preaching repentance and the baptism of repentance for the remission of sins. Andrew was accompanied by John, who later became the beloved evangelist and disciple of Christ. As the Baptist saw the Lord approaching, he pointed toward Him indicating to Andrew and John, who were apparently the Baptist's disciples, that He was "the Lamb of God, which taketh away the sin of the world" (John 1:29). Actually John, who is the only one who records this incident, does not indicate that the Lord asked Andrew and him to follow Him at this time. They were attracted to Him just by seeing Him and hearing Him converse with John the Baptist. His very presence drew them to Him. His words struck them as being, not the words of mere man, but of the incarnate Son of God, the Messiah, for whom they had been waiting so long. We read, then, in John 1:37 that they followed Him without being actually invited to do so. In fact, Christ seemed surprised when He turned around and saw them. In response to His question, "What seek ye?" they asked Him where He was staying. They called Him Teacher, Master, at first glance. The Lord said to them, "Come and see" (John 1:39). This was actually not the same imperative that the Lord gave Andrew and his brother Simon Peter later on. This experience is definitely to be distinguished from the commandment which the Lord gave to Peter and Andrew in the Synoptic Gospels. The "Come and see" of Jesus to John and Andrew was for the purpose of getting them acquainted with Him, and not equivalent to the "Follow me" of discipleship. Their following Christ in this instance was the immediate response of two seeking souls to the spoken or unspoken first commandment of Christ, "Repent ye, and believe the Gospel." The good news is here; Christ Himself is here; let's get acquainted with Him.

The Lord was not at all hesitant about having these two fishermen visit Him in His dwelling place. He was not ashamed of His poverty or His transiency. Nor should we be. It is false pride to be ashamed to invite others to visit us simply because we are poor and transient in this world. So was our Lord.

Why did John and Andrew want to visit the Lord at home? They were fishermen, but they had keen minds. They did not want just a casual conversation with the Lord Jesus but a thorough acquaintance with Him. They may have wanted to put Him to the test and find out whether He was indeed the fulfillment of prophecy. They were intelligent men, students of prophecy, who wanted their acceptance of Jesus Christ to be on an unchallengeable basis.

The best place to learn what a person is really like is in his own home. You don't know anyone well unless you have seen how he acts in his own household. It is at home that a person takes off the mask of pretense and lives his real life. That's the picture that these men wanted to get of Christ—His real self at home. We wonder, sometimes, if those who come to visit us have as good an opinion of us after they leave as when they came.

A woman and her little daughter were attending a service at which the preacher said that obedience to God is revealed by the manner in which we attend to the small duties of everyday life. He described how many parents neglect their spiritual duties in the home. The little girl listened attentively to his description of such parents, then turned to her mother and asked, "Mama, is he talking about you?" That remark pierced her heart. Remember that the first place these disciples of Christ saw Him and talked with Him was at His home. What must that home have been like? Probably there were no comfortable chairs in which to sit, but these two strangers must have stayed with the Lord quite a number of hours. Oh, if we could only remember that it is not the physical comforts of our homes that attract the best guests, but the spirit that prevails in them! It must have been in the home of Jesus, at the little village of Bethany or Bethabara by the Jordan, that He made His first two converts. Christian hospitality provides an excellent opportunity for soul-winning. In fact, one Christian missionary organization we know of specializes in this sort of evangelism. There can be nothing more Scriptural. Come and see where I stay, the Lord willingly said to the two who were so anxious to speak with Him.

What happened after this visit with the Lord Jesus? Andrew went and told his brother Peter about it, and he, too, became a beiever. But they did not quit their manual occupations as soon as they believed. They were both fishermen and from all indications they continued to go to sea. We stress this point because there are some persons who seem to think that the moment they believe on the Lord Jesus Christ they should give up their jobs and expect the ravens to feed them.

It is worthy of note that when the Lord Jesus was passing by the sea of Galilee He saw Peter and Andrew casting a net into the sea. This was their occupation and they were busy at it. We wonder if the Lord Jesus would have called them if they were just loafing around. The Lord calls busy people to work for Him, not idlers. Perhaps the Lord has saved you, but you are wondering why He has not asked you to follow Him in service. It may be that He who knows the hearts and dispositions of us all foresees that you would be a quitter instead of a worker. Perhaps He sees that you would expect Him to feed you as Elijah was fed by the ravens, while you basked in the sun of comfort and ease. Christ calls busy people and people who intend to be busy in the service of Christ. Our Master Himself was no idler. He said, "I must work the works of him that sent me, while it is day: the night cometh, when no man can work" (John 9:4).

In the life of Christ we have the highest example of a worker. When God wants a worker in His service, He calls one who is a real worker. When He has work to be done, He goes to those who are already at work. When God wants a great servant, He calls a busy man. Scripture and history attest this truth. Moses was busy with his flocks at Horeb. Saul was busy searching for his father's lost beasts. David was busy caring for his father's sheep. Elisha was busy plowing with twelve yoke of oxen. Nehemiah was busy serving as the king's cup-bearer. Amos was busy following the flock. Peter and Andrew were busy casting a net into the sea. James and John were busy mending their nets. Matthew was busy collecting taxes. Saul was busy persecuting the friends of Jesus. William Carey, the great missionary, was busy mending and making shoes.

An American was told by an English tourist that he was surprised to find no "gentlemen" in his country. "What are they?" asked the American. The Englishman replied, "People who do not work for their living." "Oh," said the American, "we have some of those here; only we call them tramps." The Lord Jesus does not ask any tramps to follow Him for service. Some of us may think we are Christian gentlemen, when in reality we are Christian tramps. Unfortunately, there are too many of these in the Kingdom of God.

If only we could all be like Sophie, the scrub woman. She was a real Christian. One of the gentlemen in the large building where she worked said to her, "Say, Sophie, I understand that you are a Christian." "Yes, sir, I am a child of the King," was her immediate reply. "Oh! So you must be a princess, since God is your King." "I sure am." "Well, if God is your Father, and you are a princess and a child of the King, don't you think that it is beneath your dignity to be found here in New York City scrubbing these dirty steps?" Nothing daunted, Sophie replied, "There is no humiliation whatsoever. You see, I'm not scrubbing these steps for Mr. Brown, my boss. I'm scrubbing them for Jesus Christ, my Saviour!"

The Lord told His disciples to pray that God might send laborers into His field, not idlers. Some well-meaning folk say, "I'll pray while you work," but in the life of our Lord prayer never took the place of work. It was at the end of a laborious day that our Lord withdrew from life to some isolated spot to pray. The two must go together in a Christian's life.

Following Christ is doing Christ's work. Andrew did not remain with Jesus but went back to fishing to make a living, and then he brought his brother Peter to Jesus. That took work. Philip followed the Saviour by bringing Nathanael. Matthew began by making a feast for his companions and introducing them to the Lord Jesus. Many Jewish rabbis preferred talkers, students, and ritualists rather than busy workers for their followers. But these proved to be false rabbis. The Lord Jesus is a working Commander, and He commands workers to come after Him. He did not care for chiefs, whose purpose in life was to be admired. He did not choose debaters, but fishermen, who through their self-sacrifice and hard work would help save the world from its blindness, sorrow, wrong, and unrighteousness. Other teachers sought holiness by separating themselves from men and by ceremonial washings and ritualistic performances. The Holy One set His disciples to seek holiness by that endless service, those grand self-denials, and that universal helpfulness, of which holiness is the ripe and precious fruit and everlasting life the glorious issue and reward.

A boy who applied for work was told by the manager that he did not think they had enough work to keep another boy busy. The boy said, "But I'm sure, sir, that you must have enough work to keep me busy. You may not know what a little amount of work it takes to keep me employed." Many so-called disciples are like this boy. They want to follow Jesus, not to see how much they can do for Him, but how little. To such the Lord never says, "Follow me." Any who enter Christian service for the sake of having an easy time will be disappointed. Christ is a busy Commander of busy soldiers.

FOLLOW CHRIST BY BEING YOURSELF

We have seen that those men whom Jesus Christ commanded to follow Him were believers and busy men. But what did He mean by the command He gave them in Mark 1:17, "Come ye after me, and I will make you to become fishers of men"?

Both Matthew and Mark use the same imperative in this call of the Lord to Peter and Andrew. The Greek word is *deute,* from the adverb *deuro,* which means "hither, here." It is the plural form of *deuro,* meaning "come," and is therefore correctly translated in the King James Version as "Come ye." The Lord Jesus saw these two fishermen fishing and making a living. He was now starting His public ministry and He needed men to help Him. He needed workers.

But we note that, before telling these men who became His apostles to go and work for Him, the Lord Jesus asked them to come and be with Him, to come after Him. He wanted them close to Himself—not that He was going to sit idly around with them, but to give them an opportunity to observe Him at work. Before they could go out to work, they had to be trained.

The Lord was always busy about His Father's business. The works He was about to perform would not only benefit others but would also strengthen the faith of the disciples. It is interesting to note that about five-sixths of the teachings of Christ were either spoken to or for the benefit of the disciples. We cannot find many public discourses of the Lord Jesus in the New Testament, but we do find an abundance of parables, conversations with His disciples, and answers to their questions. He gave Himself wholly to them, lived with, and for them, that He might make them ministers who need not be ashamed, "rightly dividing the word of truth."

The Lord Jesus' choice of men is indeed strange. It is so different from the way men would choose. He chose men we today would surely reject. The Lord does not see as man sees. He often selects men we deem unfit, and enrolls those whom the world indignantly refuses. Not one of the Twelve was either a priest or a priest's son. Not one of them belonged to the sect of the theologically sound but fanatical Pharisees. Not a tinge of clericalism was found in the whole body. The only moderately prosperous one among them was Matthew, although his income would be considered little better than average in our day. They were all provincials. None of them came from large cities. They were unlearned, poor villagers, and yet the Lord said to them, "Come ye after me."

Those whom the Lord chose were all young men. Probably He chose them young because they were more pliable and would find it easier to follow where He led. They would also have longer to serve Him. Following is an art, and there is real wisdom in the old saying, "You cannot teach an old dog new tricks." When a thoughtful child was asked why a certain tree in the garden was crooked, he said, "I suppose somebody must have stepped on it when it was a little fellow."

No doubt the Lord also called young people to follow and serve Him because they could withstand the privations that such service would entail. An old tradition tells us that the Lord once turned to His disciples and said, "The nearer you are to me the nearer you are to the fire." It is true, for nearness to Jesus always means nearness to the fire of persecution, temptation, and difficulty. The Lord Himself does not stay in the rear of the battle but leads the way. His way was the cross, and ours as His followers must be the same; but it is the cross that leads to a glorious crown.

Have you ever wondered why the Lord chose the thirtieth year of His life to launch out into His public ministry? It may have been for the same reason that He called young men to follow Him. We hear so many older people say, "I cannot take what I used to when I was young." Young men, let us be willing to take it while we are young. Following Jesus Christ means following the young Man who did not consider His youth too precious to give as a ransom for sin.

There is yet a third reason why the Lord may have called young men to follow and serve Him. In the Middle East, especially, it is never thought that a young person knows or can know as much as an older one. Age means experience, and nothing can take its place. If the Lord had called older men to follow Him, they would have thought that they knew better and could do better than He. Let us not forget that His disciples were just human beings. The Lord did not want to lead them into the temptation of misjudging their Teacher and themselves. As it was, time and again one or another of them would flame out in heated temper or a display of arrogance. And sometimes the gentlest of Teachers had to rebuke them for contentiousness. Right to the end of their special training it seemed as if they could not part with some of their false and long-cherished ambitions. Timidity was often matched by bluster, self-seeking by petty avarice, and indolence by ignorance. Just imagine how much worse it would have been if these were older people, set in their ways.

And finally, the Lord called young men because they had a long life of service before them. Since it would take Him three years or more to train them, He wanted them to have ample time to use that training. God's investment in us must be adequately realized in quality and length of service.

An amazing thing that one observes as he studies those whom Jesus called to follow Him is that they were not men who conformed to one particular rule and temperament. They were individuals and as such different. He did not ask Andrew and Peter to follow Him and then demand that all others should be possessed of exactly the same characteristics before they could do likewise. In the possession of faith, love and hope, the disciples were all alike, but in scarcely anything else. They were not imitators of one another. Christ never asks us to become duplicates of someone else. He wants us to be ourselves and follow Him alone. And though in becoming Christians, and thus becoming like Christ, we acquire many Christian principles and characteristics in common, we are still different in many, many ways. Therefore, we should not try to be Peter, or John, or Paul, or anyone else. Let us become what Christ wants us to become, like Him, and yet retaining our own individual characteristics. And it may be because of those particular, and sometimes peculiar, characteristics that He asked us to follow Him in the first place. Perhaps He has some very special use for our peculiarities, possibly to win the equally peculiar to Him.

Consider Peter. In the Bibical account of him, we see that he is ardent, impulsive, ready to strike the moment the iron is hot, and sometimes before; energetic, capable of doing a pioneer's work, a man to thrill a crowd, to launch an enterprise, or to open a new country; a born popular leader, firm as a rock, although shaken once and again to the center by the earthquake of cowardice. His brother Andrew has a herald's soul, is the first to come to Christ and the first to bring a second, and is clearly made for a courier of the advancing King. That "other disciple" —John—is meditative as a philosopher, tender as a woman, a man of sweetness and light, and yet not a weakling, but blazing out in righteous indignation, and bursting down on evil like a crushing thunderbolt. James, his senior, is his inferior in general force of nature, but has genuine power, and is one of the earliest to confess Christ, and one of the first martyrs to die for Him.

Observe the contrast in the rest of them. Philip, a matter-of-fact man, given to looking at things as they are, not to be deceived by fancies, and conquering the prejudices of his friend Nathanael, the honest, frank, and guileless Bible Student, with his one outspoken "Come and see for yourself."

Matthew, up in a moment at the Master's call, modest as a child, prompt and energetic in deed, and ready to invest his all in the golden reward of Christ's favor.

Thomas, not easily won and with difficulty retained, critical and melancholy, often whelmed by doubt and yet unquestionably loyal, a man who thinks where others feel, who cannot set his foot down till he has tested the ground beneath, believes nothing till it is proven to him, and then believes with all his soul. Verily, it has been a perpetual benediction to doubting and critical souls in all ages that Thomas was chosen by the Master and was not driven from His ranks when He was even known to have a doubt.

The third and least known quartette included James, the son of Alpheus—prudent, wise, practical, with an eye for business details and a hand to guide and rule; making with Jude, his brother, and Simon, the zealot, a triad of earnest and capable laborers for the Lord. But why the next dark and mysterious figure, that of Judas? Is he, too, to be trained to catch men: a man soon to be utterly condemned by his companions, called a thief by John, and a devil by the Lord Jesus? Yes, even he hears the word, and follows Christ! In him there are possibilities of good. He has tremendous force of will, singular energy and daring of character; and Christ, in what one calls a "high venture of that love" which hopeth all things, beholds the germ of these excellencies, and will take him and do His utmost to root out of him that mean money-greed which already threatens his destruction.

But this is not all; for Christ, as if to save us from the wretched folly that presumes on ignorance, and want of skill and power where both are to be had, completes and crowns the apostolic band by summoning to His service Saul of Tarsus, with his largely cultured nature, wide reading, massive intellect, many gifts and imperial powers, and prepares them for their highest consecration in bearing His name among the Gentiles, establishing churches in Asia and Europe, and facilitating more than any other man the preaching of His Gospel to every creature under heaven.

Thus we have every variety of original endowment, and of every bias and force, gathered in this first school of Christ. The cautious and reflective beside the impulsive and ardent; the inquiring and doubting in fellowship with the trustful and ever-believing; the ignorant and unlearned with the man of massive gifts and widest culture; the selfish and mean, smitten with the money lust, on the next form to men of self-forgetting enthusiasm, and fired with the love that gives and suffers till it can give and suffer no more. (See J. Clifford's "Christ's Training of the Ministers of the Word" in the *Christian World Pulpit,* Vol. VI, pp. 257-64.)

It is therefore more than presumption on our part to exclude any Christian from heeding the commandment of Christ to follow Him simply because he does not conform to an acceptable human formula of temperament and natural gifts. Whatever you are, once you have met Christ, follow Him. There is a place in the Kingdom of God for your ignorance and your culture, for your impulsiveness and your reticence. Christ asks us to follow Him as we are and with what we have. Don't try to make yourself over into someone else before you follow Jesus Christ.

IS CHRIST INTERESTED IN WHAT WE ARE OR WHAT WE DO?

Man loves to have a sense of direction in life. Uncertainty about the right path to take, or the proper investment of life is something all humans dread. That is why a sensible person thinks twice before making a commitment for life. If someone were to ask you to follow him just on his say-so, you wouldn't do it, would you? You would want to know him, to know why he wanted you to follow him and what his ultimate purpose was. And you would feel better about it if you were able to have a thoroughly satisfactory contract, concluded by mutual agreement and signed on the dotted line.

But when the Lord Jesus Christ called those whom He wanted to make His disciples and servants, He did not ask them to sign an agreement with Him. There can be no contract between Christ and Man—only commitment on the part of man. The Lord said, "Come ye after me, and I will make you to become fishers of men" (Mark 1:17).

The Lord never said to Peter and Andrew, or to anyone else, that they were expected to do certain specific things for Him. The Lord does not call us to follow Him for what He can get out of us but for what He can make us be. The Lord is not interested in our doings but in our beings. How much happier we would be if we only understood that following Christ is not based on a contract of works that He asks us to sign but on our willingness to yield ourselves to Him to work within us, rather than our doing something for Him. He wants to shape us into something different from what we are, at the same time using the raw material of our own personalities.

These men were fishermen. That was their vocation. That was the way they made their livelihood. To be a fisherman requires a certain amount of skill. Usually people choose the work they do because they like it and find scope in it for their particular gifts and aptitudes. If you are not happy in what you are doing, perhaps you should ask yourself if you are really doing what you should be doing. Of course, in our complex world, it is not easy to do what we like and still meet our responsibilities. It was much easier in the simple society of the first century. Our advanced civilization has not necessarily brought with it the happiness of being able to do what we want to do and are best fitted to do.

Why did the Lord tell these disciples that He would make them fishers? Because they had a natural aptitude for such work. God will use whatever we are to make us what He wants us to be. And unless we become what He wants us to be, we cannot possibly do the things He expects us to accomplish. Let us never forget that the Lord can use our natural aptitudes in our supernatural calling and work.

There is a slight variation in the wording of this call of Christ in the Gospels of Matthew and Mark. In Matthew the call is, "Follow me, and I will make you fishers of men" (4:19). In Mark it is, "Come ye after me, and I will make you *to become* fishers of men" (1:17). We should remember that the Gospel of Mark was the original Gospel that served as a reference for Matthew. And the information Mark received probably came to a great extent from Peter himself. Since this incident involves Peter directly, Mark is purposely more explicit in recording the words of Christ. He wants to make sure we realize that the Lord Jesus Christ, in calling Peter, was interested not directly in what Peter was going to do for Christ—how many souls he was going to catch in his net—but what he was going to become by following Christ. Oh, for an understanding of what Christ desires for us! He is more interested in what we are than in what we do. Sometimes we can do certain things hypocritically, without revealing our true nature. If we are not what we do, then what we do is not acceptable to Christ. It has been truly said that hypocrisy is the homage vice pays to virtue.

Christ never intended to call joiners, people who profess to follow Him but never become what He wants them to be. The classical example of a joiner is Judas, who finally betrayed Jesus Christ. The Lord knew all the time what he was and what he was going to do. But He was patient with him. There was always hope that a joiner might become a follower, that one day he would repent and believe. Oh, for joiners to understand the patience of Christ and avail themselves of it! You can be very near Christ, as Judas was; you can count yourself a disciple and be counted by others as one; yet you may not truly be a follower of Christ. Judas undoubtedly did what the other disciples were doing—they in sincerity and he in hypocrisy—but that did not make him a fisher of men. Judas was engaging in new activities right along, but he did not become a new person. He could have done so, despite the fact that his raw material was such shoddy stuff.

And this brings us to a consideration of the verb used here. "I will make you fishers of men." The word "make" in Greek is *poieesoo,* and is the word used to indicate the creative work of God. When speaking of the creation of man and woman, the Lord used the same word. "Have ye not read, that he which made them at the beginning made them male and female?" (Matt. 19:4). And the substantive *poieema,* "what is made," is used in the New Testament only of the works of divine creation. May it not be that man can be made a fisher of men only by God? And who but God in the person of the Lord Jesus Christ was speaking here? "It is not your training, or your methods, or your psychological impacts and oratorical sermons that will make you fishers of men, but I," says the Lord God, the Creator. He who made man in the beginning is the only One who can re-make him. And if we are to have any part in the capture of men and women for Jesus Christ, it has to be done in His power.

No man can become a fisher of men through his own power and choice or that of anyone else. This explains the impotence among many who are supposed to be followers of Christ and fishers of men. Some have not been fishes themselves; they have not been caught by Christ. And others still have too much of self in them. They have not yet been made fishers of men by Christ. The Lord uses this verb *poieesoo* in the first person singular future active. He does not say, "You will become," but "I will make you." The Lord is the only One who is fully justified in using this verb in the first person singular. He is God and is entitled to say "I," for without Him we could be absolutely nothing.

It would have been a perfectly good Greek construction for Mark to say, "Come after me, and ye shall become fishers of men." But he does not say that. He says, "Come ye after me, and *I will make you* to become fishers of men." It is not the following that makes us fishers of men, but Christ Himself. Nothing we do in respect to God results in recreating us and transforming us. The process by which God works is for us to place ourselves at the disposal of Christ, who in turn makes us channels fit for His use. Neither we nor anything we do will make us fishers of men. You know that it is possible for us to fish and yet not be fishermen. It is possible for us to be preachers and yet not to have been transformed by the power of God into real fishermen, into God's creation. Before we can do what He wants us to do, we must allow Him to make us what He desires us to be. As a great man of God said, "The Lord Jesus Christ has been handicapped by His connection with His followers." I must examine my own soul and life to see whether this is true of me. Will you do the same?

DEPENDENT AND YET INDEPENDENT

Come ye after me, and I will make you to become fishers of men" (Mark 1:17). These words were spoken to the ones whom the Lord Jesus intended to become His apostles during His earthly life and after His return to heaven. These people were to enter the ministry of the Gospel.

Naturally, since this was the beginning of the Christian era, there were no theological schools to which they could go for training, nor any teachers to instruct them. Therefore, the Lord Jesus Christ, both in His humanity and deity, had to act as their sole teacher. But what a teacher they had! The ministry of the apostles did not really start until after the Lord Jesus had ascended into heaven. The time of His public ministry among them was actually the time of their training, and we may well assume that one of the main reasons for what Christ did and said during that period was the instruction of His followers. This is evidenced by the fact, mentioned previously, that five-sixths of all the teachings of Christ were spoken either to or for the disciples. Their theological seminary was their constant fellowship with the Lord Jesus Christ for nearly three and a half years. The Lord rarely worked a miracle or spoke to the multitudes without the presence of some of His disciples. With the exception of His frequent retirements at night for prayer and communion with God the Father, the Lord Jesus was to be found with those whom He had called to follow Him.

Mark contributes something significant here. "And he [Christ] ordained twelve, that they should be with him, and that he might send them forth to preach" (3:14). It is interesting to note that the verb "ordained" used by Mark is exactly the same as that used by the Lord when He called His disciples: "I will make you [*poieesoo*] to become fishers of men."

The verb in Mark 3:14 is *epoieesen,* the same verb in the first aorist. The primary meaning of the word is "to make." This agrees perfectly with all that we have said in our previous study concerning the reshaping of the lives of those whom the Lord calls to serve Him. Mark 3:14 could very well, and in fact more accurately, be translated, "And he made twelve that they may be with him, and so that he may keep sending them to preach and to have authority to cast out demons." How does the Lord make a disciple, an apostle, a preacher? By inviting them to be with Him. They must learn of Him before they can be sent forth to preach.

This Greek word *poieeoo,* "to make," found in Mark 1:17 and 3:14, was used in classical Greek to bring out the object and end of an act. The Lord desired the salvation of men. He came to seek and to save that which was lost. The aim of His disciples and apostles should certainly be the same as His. The object and end of the fellowship to which the Lord invited them was to make them fishers of men. It was not to make them feel happy and secure under the wings of the incarnate God, but to accomplish in them what was necessary for them to accomplish the work of God. The salvation of men and women from sin is Christ's primary objective, and this should be the main purpose of every follower of Christ. Our object as His disciples should not be the organization of a system of theological thought, or the defense and propagation of our own particular church or denomination, but the salvation of souls from the guilt and penalty of sin. Christ called the disciples in order to make them fishers of men. This was His paramount effort as He came into contact with multitudes as with individuals. Study carefully Christ's way with men and you will see that His primary concern was to reconcile them with God their Creator. Everything else took second place.

To enjoy fellowship with Christ for its own sake is good but it is even better to recognize it as a time of preparation for passing the blessing along to needy souls we shall meet along the way. Even in our fellowship with God there should be no selfish motive. Our facing God in His holiness should be the preparation for our facing men in their sin. And only as we do it in this order shall we be successful fishers of men.

Mountain-top experiences are good, but let's not forget that after having them we must descend to the valley of human despair and need. At one of Mr. Moody's meetings a man rose to give his testimony. "I have been for five years on the Mount of Transfiguration," he began. Instantly Mr. Moody interrupted him with the question, "How many souls did you lead to Christ last year?" "Well, I don't know," answered the surprised man. "Have you led any?" Mr. Moody pursued further. "I-er-don't know that I have," stammered the man. "Then," snapped Mr. Moody sternly, "we don't want that kind of mountain-top experience. When a man gets so high that he can't reach down and save poor sinners, there is something wrong."

Mr. Moody tells of seeing a steel engraving one day that pleased him very much. He says, "I thought it was the finest thing I had ever seen, at the time, and I bought it." It was the picture of a woman coming up out of the water and clinging with both hands to the Cross of Refuge. "But afterward," he goes on to say, "I saw another picture which spoiled this one for me entirely—it was so much more lovely. It was a picture of a person coming out of the dark waters with one arm clinging to the Cross; but with the other she was lifting someone else out of the waves." That is what the Lord Jesus meant His followers to be: disciples who put communion with God first, but for the express purpose of rescuing others from sin and death. Christ's desire was, in the words of A. B. Bruce, "not only to have disciples, but to have about Him men whom he might train to make disciples of others: to cast the net of divine truth into the sea of the world, and to land on the shores of the divine kingdom a great multitude of believing souls." (*The Training of the Twelve,* p. 13.)

There is another particular meaning to this verb *poieeoo,* "to make." It refers to the producing and bringing forth of something that, upon being produced, has an independent existence of its own, as *poiein paidion,* "making of a child." The child made by a woman has an independent existence from the mother, although its existence is derived from the mother. The same thing is true of a tree making fruit. The fruit is the product of the tree, but it has independent existence from the tree. (See R. C. Trench, *Synonyms of the New Testament,* p. 361.)

This shows that, although the purpose of the disciples of Christ is one—that of fishing for men—their personalities are diverse. They are independent of Christ in that they cannot assume His identity or do the work that belongs exclusively to Him. They can, for instance, point men and women to the Lamb of God who takes away the sin of the world, but they can never rightfully claim that they can take away men's sins themselves. When we are with Christ, and are made His disciples—His fishers of men—that does not mean that we are made Christ Himself and can assume His power and prerogatives. We must understand our limitations as human beings; we can never be what our Master is, or do what He alone can do. We are independent of Him, yet fully dependent upon Him, because we cannot be what He is or do what He does. Therefore our independence does not exclude our dependence upon Him, even as the fruit of the tree cannot claim its absolute independence from the tree that produced it. Fruit is used for feeding and nourishing human beings, but it would not be there if it were not for the tree. The tree does something which the fruit cannot do, and the fruit does something which the tree cannot do directly. This helps to illustrate the independence of the fisher of men from Christ and yet the interdependence of one on the other.

Again—each piece of fruit on a tree is similar to every other piece, but there is no absolute identity among them. The basic elements are the same, but there are differences in appearance, taste, and value. So it is with us, who are the fruit of fellowship with Christ. We cannot all be identical. Some of us are "juicy" and some of us rather dry; some of us are long and some are short on certain characteristics; some of us are aggressive and some of us are quiet. We are different, and yet our aim should always be the same—the leading of souls to Jesus Christ. Even the fruit we produce by His power is different, but it is still fruit.

SHOULD A CHRISTIAN GIVE UP HIS JOB IN ORDER TO FOLLOW CHRIST?

What should a Christian do about his way of life when he hears the call of Christ to follow Him? Should he resign his secular job, forsake his family, and separate himself from the world in which he lives? Does following Christ mean being with Him alone and ceasing to be with men? Does doing His work mean not doing any secular work to earn one's daily living? Just what is involved in following Christ?

As we face this realistic issue of life as Christians, let us look back and see what the disciples did when the Lord Jesus called them to go after Him. Both Matthew and Mark agree on this point. "And straightway they left their nets, and followed him" (Matt. 4:20, cf. Mark 1:18). In Luke 5:11 the reaction to such a call from the Lord on the part of some of the disciples was, "And when they had brought their ships to land, they forsook all, and followed him." But as we pointed out in a previous study, this seems to be a different occasion from the one referred to by Matthew and Mark.

For a whole year, Andrew and Simon followed the Lord Jesus in His ministry, observing His deeds and words, before they received this specific call to follow Him in service. During this time they had not given up their employment as fishermen. Nor was this call to fellowship their call to become of the number of the twelve apostles. This latter call came some months later and is recorded in Matthew 10:1-4, Mark 3:13-19, and Luke 6:13-17. The present call was for them to follow Jesus with a view to later becoming "fishers of men," that is, to leave their occupation and become permanent disciples, and thus be instructed and trained for the work of preaching the Gospel.

But the question is, Who supported them while they were following the Lord Jesus Christ? He did not have any money or material resources to supply their physical needs. Was He such an idealist that He would completely disregard the bodily needs of the disciples who gave themselves to Him for training? There was no missionary society to support them, as no church had yet been established.

In Matthew 8:14, Mark 1:29, and Luke 4:38, we read of the Lord Jesus entering Simon Peter's house and healing his mother-in-law of a fever. This indicates that Simon and Andrew, whom the Lord had previously called, still owned their own house. It is certainly no sin to own your own house, if that does not become your idol and your god. The home of these disciples was no hindrance to their following the Lord. What is actually meant by the necessity of our leaving "all" (whether this is a house, or a father and mother, brothers and sisters, sons and daughters) to follow Jesus is not the reckless abandonment of relatives and possessions, but not allowing anything to interfere with our following Christ faithfully.

In addition to being an idealist, the Lord Jesus was also a realist. His idealism never conflicted with His realism. He knew that one must eat to live, and He Himself did eat. The Scriptures, however, are silent on how the Lord was sustained physically during the time of His public ministry. Up to the thirtieth year of His life, He worked as a carpenter in Nazareth. He was not idle. But after that? Undoubtedly He must have partaken of food, because He was accused of being a glutton and a drinker, not necessarily because He ate and drank too much, that is, more than necessary, but because He ate and drank at all and sometimes in the company of notorious sinners. Perhaps men felt that He who claimed to be God incarnate should not need to eat, even as some folk today seem to feel that, since we as Christians are supposed to live by faith, we should wait for the ravens of heaven to feed us, or we should completely disregard the needs of our bodies. But there is ample evidence that the Lord Himself did not. He was also a man just like us, with the exception that He had no sin in Himself.

When Peter and Andrew heard the call of Christ to follow Him, it is not necessary to suppose they actually gave up all their property. But Scripture says, "And straightway they left their nets, and followed him." It is important to note that the main verb in this verse is not "left" but "followed." The word "left" in the original Greek is a participle, *aphentes,* "having left." The leaving of the nets was incidental to the main act of following Jesus Christ. It is as if we are told here that the disciples did not permit their nets, with which they were working, to become an obstacle in following Jesus Christ. And this is the general lesson that we must all learn. Absolutely nothing should hinder us from following Christ. Whatever tends to do this must be left behind. That which enables us to earn a living must become incidental to our fidelity in following and obeying Christ.

But does leaving the nets behind indicate that the disciples actually gave up their claim of ownership? We seriously doubt that. Peter and Andrew were professional fishermen, who fished primarily in the Sea of Galilee. Josephus, the Jewish historian who at one time was governor of Galilee, tells us that in his day three hundred and thirty fishing boats sailed the waters of this lake. And how big do you think it was? Thirteen miles long by eight miles wide. It is called by three names: the Sea of Galilee, the Sea of Tiberias, and the Lake of Gennesaret. It lies in a dip in the earth's surface 680 feet below sea level. Naturally it has a tropical climate. Although now it is almost deserted, in the days of the Lord Jesus it had nine townships clustered round its shores, none of them with fewer than 15,000 people. In a place like that, Peter and Andrew could not have been fishing alone. There were other fishermen there, for fish was the staple diet of the people of Palestine. (See Matt. 7:10; Mark 6:30-44; Luke 11:11; 24:42.) They ate meat only once a week. Fishing was in important business. Some of the names of the towns by the lakeside indicate this. Bethsaida, for instance, means The House of Fish. Tarichaea, another lakeside town, means The Place of Salt Fish, and it was there that fish was preserved for export to Jerusalem and Rome.

Andrew and Peter, two of the first believers on the Lord Jesus Christ, were fishing. We are told that they were casting the net. In Greek, the word for "net" is *amphibleestron,* which means a small net skillfully cast into the water by hand. It was shaped rather like an umbrella, and as it was drawn through the water it caught and enclosed the fish. There was also in use another kind of larger net called *sageenee,* a kind of seine or trawl, which was let out from the end of the boat. It was an *amphibleestron,* a small net cast from the shore, that Peter and Andrew had. They looked up and saw Christ approaching. They were acquainted with Him. He said to them, "Come ye after me, and I will make you to become fishers of men." Their immediate reaction was to do so. But would they abandon their net? They did not want to carry it with them. They wanted to follow Jesus unencumbered. But we don't believe that the Lord

Himself would have thought much of them if they had just gone off and left it on the shore. They probably asked one of their fellow fishermen, or even the father of James and John (Matt. 4:22), to take care of their net while they were gone. This would have been the most natural thing to do. Christ never condones the waste of material or spiritual possessions. He wants them to be used for His glory. It is unjustified, then, to assume that the disciples here abandoned their net absolutely, since it was the means of their livelihood.

When we read of the calling of John and James in Matthew 4:21, 22 and Mark 1:19, 20, we find that these two "left their father Zebedee in the ship with the hired servants, and went after him." There was no unwise abandonment of property but rather an arrangement for its further use, without allowing it to interfere with the desire to follow the Master.

Did they use this net in the days to come, in the next two years or so? We are not told. But surely they must have. In Matthew 17:24-27, we find the tax-collectors coming to Peter and asking him whether his Master paid taxes. The Lord, it may be to teach Peter by an object lesson of His divine omniscience, told him to cast a hook in the sea and catch a fish, in whose mouth he would find a coin which he was to pay to the local revenue agents for both of them. Casting a hook to catch fish was still something that came very naturally to Peter.

But surely Andrew and Peter never permitted the earning of a livelihood to interfere with their fellowship with the Lord, or their training for His service, or their service itself. The two can go together perfectly well. The followers of Christ do not have to depend on gifts while others depend on the sweat of their brow. This does not refer to those who are called into full-time service for the Lord. We shall have more to say about them in our next study.

FOLLOWING CHRIST AT PERSONAL DISADVANTAGE

One day the Lord Jesus borrowed a fisherman's boat in which to stand up and address the multitudes upon the shore of the Lake of Galilee. When He had finished speaking, He turned to Peter, whose boat He had used, and told him to row out into the deep part of the lake and let down his net. Peter was astonished at the great netfull of fish he caught, but Jesus said to him, "Fear not; from henceforth thou shalt catch men" (Luke 5:10).

Matthew and Mark give us Christ's original call to Andrew and Peter. This incident in Luke happened upon a later occasion, on which the Lord was dealing with Peter, who had already been called and was aware of his call. Through the miracle described in Luke, the Lord assured Peter that he was going to catch an abundance of men, even as at the command of Christ he had caught so many fishes. This was prophetic of the Day of Pentecost, when Peter caught 3,000 people in the net of the Gospel, as they believed on the Lord Jesus Christ through his preaching.

Note that Peter is still using his boat, in Luke 5:1-11, after his original call as recorded in Matthew and Mark. He had not sold either his boat or his net. He had left them temporarily to follow Christ, but he came back to them and earned his living by manual labor. It is inconceivable that Peter or any of the disciples ever became a financial liability to Christ and His cause. What a lesson for us to learn. Perhaps Peter and Andrew were even able to donate some of the proceeds from their fishing, from time to time, to the Lord.

In Luke's account we read that the Lord commanded Peter, who had failed in his fishing the previous night, to try again. Christ is not satisfied to see a Christian fail in business. He wants us to be diligent in our work. He more or less gave direction to Peter's casting of the net. Christ became a partner, so to speak, in Peter's business. And it was a tremendous success. The same thing happened to his business partners, James and John. But in Luke 5:11 we read again, "They, having left all, followed him" (literal translation). Are we to understand by this that all the fish they caught were left to rot on the beach while they followed Jesus? Hardly. No doubt they were left with John and James' father, Zebedee, and the hired fishermen of whom mention is made. No, business went on as before, far more successfully as Christ was made a partner in it and as long as it was not allowed in any way to interfere with their fellowship with Him. The Lord Jesus does not bring about the abolition of business, but blessing to it, as long as we make it only a means to an end and not the end in itself. Living is not just working, but working helps us to live in such a way as to glorify the Lord Jesus Christ.

Following Christ means living with Him, which in no way precludes our working to make a living. Why should anyone be ashamed of being a businessman as he lives and works for Christ? Paul made tents. On the other hand, we are not to criticize those who are so busy for Christ that they live by the Gospel. Paul said it, although he preferred not to practice it: "Even so hath the Lord ordained that they which preach the gospel should live of the gospel" (I Cor. 9:14). But preaching must be real work and not merely an excuse for it.

A similar incident, which occurred after the resurrection of the Lord Jesus Christ, is recorded in John 21:1-14. Here we find Peter declaring to the other disciples by the sea that he was going fishing. He was joined by the others. They had not forgotten their trade, for they had not given it up entirely.

They gave it up only insofar as it proved a hindrance to them in following Christ. But it is apparent that in their following of Him they kept on fishing in order to supply their daily needs.

Christ in calling us to follow Him does not want us to become financial liabilities to Him, but rather financial assets. And this can be done without any conflict. There can be harmony between the spiritual and the material, between idealism and realism in life. An understanding of this is essential if we are going to give the world a true picture of Christ and His provision for our life, life which consists of both body and spirit.

It is significant to note that, immediately after this incident in which the risen Lord, having eaten with His disciples, spoke to Peter for what was probably the last time here on earth, He again asked him to follow Him. In John 21:19, the Lord said to Peter, "Follow me." The commandment which He had given him at the beginning, He repeated at the end of His public ministry. Peter was already a follower of Christ when the Lord told him again to follow Him. But he had often failed Him, even as you and I, he was the only one who had the courage to enter the courtyard while Christ was being tried, yet he denied the Lord three times. Peter's following of Christ was imperfect because he was an imperfect man, even though he had been saved by Christ.

The Greek form of the commandment in John 21:19 is *akolouthei moi,* "Follow me." It uses the second person, singular, present imperative of the verb *akoloutheoo,* which in no way implies that Peter's following of Christ, imperfect though it was, had been interrupted. We could just as well translate this commandment, "Keep on following me."

But where would Peter's following lead him now? The Lord Jesus reissued His command to Peter after His redemptive death on the cross and the glory of the resurrection, intimating to Peter that this was where he should be ready to follow Him. Christ predicted a martyr's death for Peter, but it would be followed by a crown on the resurrection day. When Peter first heard the Lord Jesus saying to him and Andrew, "Follow me, and I will make you fishers of men," he was not fully aware of the natural consequences involved. Catching men is a far greater task than catching fish. Perhaps Peter thought of it as a promotion, the realization of his youthful vocational dream. It was even worth leaving his nets for. A glorious prospect lay before him.

Again, he may have thought that Christ would establish a political kingdom. Peter had seen the Lord perform miracles and he was persuaded that the establishment of His earthly kingdom was only a matter of time. So when Christ asked Peter to follow Him, he may have thought of himself as a potentially big wheel in the coming Messianic government. A bit of selfishness may have crept into his willingness to follow Christ.

But now he is asked to continue following the Lord even to the cross, for the cross leads to the resurrection. His discipleship of over two years had not resulted in any political or economic advantages. And now he learns that if he really loves his Master and wants to continue following Him to the very end, it may lead to the cross. If he is not willing to do this, even the forsaking of his nets is of no real value.

It is significant that the love which the Lord demands of Peter in this 21st chapter of John is the Greek *agapee.* The first two times He asks "Lovest thou me?" (vv. 15, 16), He uses the verb *agapas,* which conveys the idea of loving someone, not for what you can get out of him, but despite the disadvantages association with him may bring. But Peter was too honest to say that he loved the Lord in such an unselfish and self-sacrificing spirit. In his reply, he used the verb *phileoo,* which lacks the higher characteristics of *agapaoo.* The Lord wanted Peter to love Him, not for benefits he expected to receive from Christ, but in spite of the fact that following Him would lead to the cross.

Very little in the way of sacrifice of material gain may be asked of the great majority of those who follow the Lord Jesus. However, a far weightier "Follow me" may be addressed to followers of experience like Peter, where the following leads to the sacrifice of life itself, if need be, on the altar of service.

GAINS AND LOSSES IN FOLLOWING CHRIST

In deciding whether to obey the call of Christ to follow Him and become fishers of men, we may be sure that nothing we leave behind, no matter how precious it seems, can compare with what we have and become in Christ.

The readiness with which Peter and Andrew obeyed Christ is most unusual. We are told that they left their nets immediately. Christ fascinated them. He filled them with expectations such as they had never known before. Man is incurably fascinated with the future. The present is never as satisfying as the possibilities of the days and years ahead. The Lord here presented these fishermen with the brightest of prospects for the future.

It is probable that a great deal more was said between the disciples and the Lord Jesus than is recorded in this encounter. We have only a brief account of it. The details are not necessary. All the Holy Spirit wants us to know is that the Lord Jesus issued the call and these men accepted it without reservation.

It was this that immortalized them. Today, more than 1900 years after these men accepted the call of Christ, they are more famous than the emperors of Rome or the scholars and sculptors of Greece. Few know who built the Parthenon, but millions know who Peter and Andrew were. The name of Caesar is not as widely known as that of the fishermen Peter and Andrew. There have been great generals like Napoleon; great religious reformers like Luther, Savonarola, and Wycliffe; great poets like Dante and Milton; great orators like Demosthenes and Cicero; great philosophers like Socrates and Kant. The fame of none is so widely extended, and among the best and most intelligent people of the earth, as that of these fishermen of Galilee. Their accepting this call immortalized them. Their placing their business in second place and Christ in first place wrote their names indelibly in the annals of history. Men who seek greatness for the sake of greatness may float to the top either through human ingenuity or trickery, but the day comes when they have to die, and once they sink involuntarily they sink forever. Real and lasting greatness comes to those who unreservedly obey the Lord, not for the sake of becoming great, but of becoming humble servants of a great God. The Lord seeks such to follow Him. Are you one of them?

Above all, we must understand that what we lose in following Christ is far smaller than what we gain in Him and through Him. How small-minded Peter was when he said to Christ, "Behold, we have forsaken all, and followed thee; what shall we have therefore?" (Matt. 19:27; cf. Mark 10:28, Luke 18: 28). Peter was very human, like you and me. When we respond to the call of Christ and follow Him, we think we have given up a great deal. We look at the world and measure what we have with what we could have had. After all, look at how many rich people have made great fortunes because they had no principles to hinder them. Look what it has cost us to follow Christ. Is that what is in your mind? If so, you are on dangerous ground. Listen to what the Lord said to Peter and to us: "Verily I say unto you, There is no man that hath left house, or brethren, or sisters, or father, or mother, or wife, or children, or lands, for my sake, and the gospel's, but he shall receive an hundredfold now in this time, houses, and brethren, and sisters, and mothers, and children, and lands, with persecutions; and in the world to come eternal life" (Mark 10:29, 30).

A godly old man was walking along the road from his farm to the church one day, reading his New Testament as he went. A friend met him and said, "Good morning, Mr. Price." "Ah, good morning," replied the farmer. "I am reading my Father's will as I walk along." "Oh? What has He left you?" asked his friend. "Why, He has bequeathed me a hundredfold more in this life, and in the world to come everlasting life."

Before you think of the losses that have come to you as a result of following Christ, examine the joys you have experienced. Look at what He has done for you and see whether what you have done for Him can compare with that. When you realize the blessings of following Christ, you will never think of the losses incurred on the way. When Christ has first place in your life, nothing that you leave behind will be considered loss. The houses, the family, the nets, the business, everything else takes its rightful place and is used to accomplish its God-appointed purpose, the glory of Christ. Putting things in their right perspective is truly following Christ. Abandoning things for His sake, so that you may some day boast, "Look at all I have left behind for the sake of Christ," is really no sacrifice at all. The full benefit of following Christ comes when you realize first what He has done for you and then what you can do for Him.

There is an old Dutch picture of a little child letting go of a beautiful toy. Looking at the painting, one is surprised to see the plaything so carelessly abandoned, until, following the child's glance to the upper corner of the picture one sees a lovely white dove flying down into his outstretched hands. That is the way it will be with us as soon as we actually begin to see the pure beauties and joys of the higher life. All our foolish playthings will be allowed to fall out of our hands. We shall let go of fashion and luxury, of idle dissipation and proud ambition, of greed for gain and desire for men's applause, and for advancement in the world, and we shall stretch out our hands for the things that are truly worth having.

Those are the things that will stay with us. They will impart something of their nature to our lives, and will ennoble everything they touch.

In this calling of the disciples, our Lord wanted to teach us that those who follow Him are to turn their attention from material things to human beings. Our sense of values must be changed. Things are to serve men, not to become their masters. That is why the Lord used the expression, "And I will make you to become fishers of men." While you are using things as a means to an end, never lose sight of the end—the human beings who are all around you. You must catch fish in order to live, but catching men so that they may experience life everlasting, life more abundant, is more important. Don't do the one and leave the other undone. Life must be more than fishing for a living. It must mean making it worth living for others. What we ourselves have experienced in Christ, we must share with others, that they may experience it, too. Following Christ means acquiring a balanced sense of values with regard to human lives and the material means to sustain them.

When we win a soul for Christ, can we compare that experience with anything the world has to offer in the way of fame or wealth? When we love Christ, we must love people—not things. And we come to love people because we love Christ. If we do not love those whom we see how can we prove that we love God whom we do not see? A man in whose eyes men are not precious can hardly be said to be a follower of Christ.

To see a person come to Christ as the result of our witness, by word, pen, or life, is an incomparable experience. A girl in a mission school sang all day as she went about her tasks. When asked why she was so happy, she said, "I have been redeemed from idolatry, and you can never know what that means. I am at liberty. It is like slipping suddenly from midnight darkness into brightest noontide of glory." If that was the experience of this girl, can you imagine the joy of the one who led her to Christ? The simple joy of the person who finds his liberty in the net of Christ is great, but the joy of the fisherman who catches him in the net is compounded. The Lord invites us to place ourselves at His disposal so that He can make us fishers of men, thus enabling us to have compounded joy—the joy not simply of being caught, but of catching others.

RUB SHOULDERS WITH LIFE WHILE FOLLOWING CHRIST

Why did the Lord call fishermen to follow Him? Why not shepherds? True, the Lord, just before He ascended into heaven, did tell Peter to feed His sheep. But when He first called him and his brother Andrew, He chose them as fishermen and He meant them to continue as fishermen until they could do the work of shepherds.

The shepherd in the East was the symbol of bravery and devotion. Jesus did not present Himself as the chief fisherman but as the Good Shepherd. In the Old Testament, many of God's chosen men were shepherds. Among them were Abraham, Isaac, Jacob, Moses, and David. The birth of Christ in Bethlehem was first announced to shepherds. How strange for the Lord Jesus, then, not to include shepherds among His twelve disciples. Was this merely a result of chance or was it done by design? No act of Christ's, no choice of His, is the result of chance. Surely it was a purposeful choice—this calling of the fishermen—by which Christ wanted to give us an insight into what He considers important and also indicate the way in which we should follow Him.

This choice of fishermen was also a fulfillment of prophecy. In Jeremiah 16:16 the Lord says, "Behold, I will send for many fishers, saith the Lord, and they shall fish them." And then Ezekiel 47:10 speaks of the fishers who would gather exceeding many fish.

It was not because there were no shepherds available that Christ chose fishermen. But shepherds live in the mountains, with only their sheep for company. They have little contact with their fellow men. A fisherman, on the other hand, cannot very well carry on his profession by himself. Of necessity he mixes with people. He must deal with the boatmen in order to buy or rent a boat. He must also buy nets. In the market place he must compete with others in the selling of his fish. Men do not gather around a shepherd when he enters town, but they do run to see what the fisherman has caught. Following Christ in no way means isolation. He never meant for us to follow Him in a monastery, secluded from and unaffected by the world to transform the world for Him. The Lord never called anyone to follow Him by taking up a monastic life.

Luther, who was saved from a life of monasticism and self-affliction, said, "More and greater sins are committed when men are alone than when they keep themselves in fellowship. When Eve in paradise walked alone, then came the evil one and deceived her. Whoever is among honest men and in honest company, is ashamed to sin; or, at least he has no place or opportunity to do so. When King David was alone and idle, and did not go out into the wars, he fell into adultery and murder; and I have myself found that I have never fallen into more sin than when I was alone. Solitariness invites melancholy; and a person alone has often some heavy and evil thoughts, so hath he strange thoughts, and construes everything in the worse sense. Melancholy is an instrument of the devil, by which he accomplishes his wicked purposes. The deeper a person is plunged into that state, the more power the devil has over him. To live in an open, public state, is the safest. Openly, and among other persons, a man must live civilly and honestly—must appear to fear God, and do his duty toward men."

The Lord chose fishermen, then, because He did not want secluded men for His disciples but those who mingled with others in everyday life. Today Jesus does not seek those who retire from the world, but Christians in the market place, the office, the factory. Rubbing shoulders with the world is necessary if we are to win the world to Christ. We must go where the fish are, for they will never come to us.

Once you become a child of God through regeneration, you must also become a fisherman. This does not mean leaving your present position and retiring from the world, but becoming a fisher of men for Christ wherever you are. It is sad when those who receive the Lord Jesus Christ as their Saviour cannot get along with their fellow workers, family, and friends. Of course, they must take their stand for the Lord Jesus Christ and His principles, but they should not become offensive to such a degree that others do not want to be around them, or so wise in their own conceits that they do not want to be around others. When we become born-again Christians, we must guard against becoming so individualistic and self-confident about our knowledge and sufficiency in Christ that we want to stand above others or not associate with them at all.

The Lord Jesus Christ may have chosen fishermen instead of shepherds because fishermen know how to work together with others, while shepherds are more independent and authoritarian. The shepherd is alone with his sheep and imposes his will upon them. He is a stranger to the art of group life, of cooperation. But if a fisherman does not learn to work with others, he will die of hunger. Individualism in a fisherman would prove his ruin. Unfortunately there are too many shepherds in the family of Christ and not enough fishermen. Individualism rather than cooperation prevails among our leaders. The work of Christ is not achieved by the imposed will of the few upon the many, but by the cooperation of Christ's common fishermen in bringing about His will. He is the Shepherd; we are only fishermen. Let us not forget this.

In Mark 9:38-40, we read of certain disciples who wanted a monopoly on the business of casting out evil. They resented it when a free-lance Christian, without an official license, did good works in Jesus' name. The centuries have passed, but there are still many Christians who would like to silence groups other than their own. Some denominations think that they have a monopoly on doing things for Christ, and, like the disciples of old, would put other denominations out of business if they could.

A preacher who spoke to large congregations every Sunday was twitted by another for not being "in the line of apostolic succession." "That does not worry me," the brother replied, "as long as I am having apostolic success." And such apostolic success comes when we learn to work together with Christ and with other fishermen in a tumultuous sea. The fish will be frightened away by fishermen who fight each other, but can be readily caught by those who in quiet cooperation and mutual respect cast their nets into the sea.

There is an old legend about a herd of mules that was attacked nightly by a pack of wolves from a nearby forest. When the wolves came, the mules began kicking viciously in all directions. Consequently the mules maimed and injured each other, while the agile wolves escaped unharmed. Finally, a wise mule called the rest together for a conference and made known his plans. That night the wolves came yelping from the forest as usual but, instead of the mules kicking promiscuously, they all ran and put their heads together in a circle and began kicking outward. The wolves were put to flight and the mules did no harm to each other. Christians need to get their heads together and kick outward against the forces of iniquity. The world must sometimes wonder whether we who call ourselves Christ's fishermen have any heads to put together.

It is the work of the shepherd to protect and care for his sheep, but the job of the fisherman is to go where the fish are and catch them. The one is a guardian, the other a hunter. It is the primary duty of every Christian to be a fisher of souls.

No one can become a shepherd in the service of Christ who is not first of all a fisherman. Men must first be caught for Christ before they can be nurtured. The Lord wants us first to be fishers and then shepherds. In the Scriptures, the Lord's call to become fishers of men was more general and wide than His call to feed sheep. We need many fishers and few shepherds. Had Peter not been a fisherman first, the Lord would never have asked him, toward the end of His earthly sojourn, to feed His sheep. Peter was a fisherman who became a shepherd, but when he became a shepherd he did not stop his work as a fisherman. How we need shepherds in our time who begin with fishing and never cease to be fishermen, even while they continue to nurture and build up the Church of Christ.

GO WHERE THE FISH ARE

What is the primary concern of a fisherman? To find pleasure in the sea? Of course not. He goes to sea because that is where the fish are. This is the first lesson a follower of Christ who would fish for men must learn: our sea is the world in which we live, but we are not here primarily to enjoy the world but to fish in it. We must work in the world but not allow the world to work in us. A ship is in its rightful place in the water, but if the water gets into the ship, down it goes. The attitude of a fisherman toward the sea is entirely different from that of a visitor or vacationer. The fish are just about the only thing that a fisherman can see in the sea, while the vacationer appreciates its pleasure-giving aspects. We are supposed to be fishermen in this world and not vacationers. We must seek to deliver the men in the world who are bound by it and its pleasures, instead of enjoying the pleasures that have bound them.

A man who was considering the claims of Christianity bemoaned the lot that would be his if he gave himself to Christ. "I shall have to give up so much!" he said. "There are many things I can do now that I could not do then." "But," said a Christian brother, "there are many things that you can't do now. You cannot eat mud or drink it." "No," replied the man, "but I don't want to do a thing like that." "That's just it," his friend said. "When you become a thorough-going Christian, all sin and the pleasures of the world will become distasteful to you. You will not want to indulge in them." This is what happens when real followers of Christ become fishers of men. They look upon the sea for the fish it contains, not for the pleasure it affords.

A good fisherman becomes well acquainted with the sea. He knows that fish are not found in all parts of it. He must know where to find the fish before he can attempt to catch them. To throw his net at random would be foolish and unjustifiably expensive. He must also be willing to learn from others where the fish are. The sea of life is so vast and the fish are so numerous that no one can rightfully claim that there is nothing he can do. There are fish somewhere, if one will only look for them. The Lord demonstrated this to Peter on several occasions when, after laboring all night, he could not catch anything. When the Lord told him where to cast his net, the catch was greater than his net could bear. In fishing for souls, we must seek the guidance and direction of the Master Fisherman, the Lord Jesus Himself, as well as those who are experienced at this divine art.

A priest had a striking dream. He thought that he had ascended the ladder that reached from earth to heaven. Expectantly he knocked upon the door, and a voice demanded, "Who is there?" Proudly the priest called out his name. "Who is with you?" was the next question. "No one," answered the priest. "I am alone." "Sorry," said the admitting angel, "but we are instructed never to open these gates for a single individual." Crestfallen and disappointed, he returned to earth. Of course, the theology of the dream is not correct, because our personal redemption does not depend upon our leading someone to Jesus Christ. But this dream did impress upon the priest the importance of leading others to the Lord. Certainly no one can give the excuse that there are no fish in the sea. It is up to us to cast our nets where the fish are.

A fisherman who tries one spot for a while and does not catch anything will move on to another spot. Christians should not sit down and bemoan the fact that there are no fish in their locality, but move on to where the fish are more abundant. This is what the Lord meant when He said, "And whosoever shall not receive you, nor hear your words, when ye depart out of that house or city, shake off the dust of your feet" (Matt. 10:14). And again our Lord spoke about this in no uncertain terms when He said, "Give not that which is holy unto the dogs, neither cast ye your pearls before swine, lest they trample them under their feet, and turn again and rend you" (Matt. 7:6). Fishermen, cast your nets where you are most likely to catch fish.

The fish will never come to the fisherman—quite the contrary. It is the fisherman who must go after the fish. That is the trouble with much Christian work nowadays. We establish a Gospel center, a church, a mission, and there we wait for people to come and hear the Gospel. Sadly enough, very few come; usually the same ones over and over again. The greatest part of this world's population has never come under the sound of the Gospel even once. Who ever heard of the fish going looking for the hook? Who ever heard of a sinner going looking for a Saviour? The whole tenor of the New Testament is that of a Saviour coming to seek and to save that which was lost. We Christians are afraid of the world and its contaminating power. We are afraid of the sea because we might get dirty and wet. We want the fish to come out of the sea to us. But they won't. We must seek them.

We must bring the Gospel to the world in such a way that they cannot possibly escape it. The Lord gave me a vision of how to do this for all the Greek-speaking people of the world: by publishing Gospel messages every week as paid advertisements in their secular newspapers and magazines. One of these is a love story magazine full of sexy stories and pictures that no decent Christian would look at. Yet over 100,000 young people read it for enjoyment. It would be almost impossible to get these young people to attend a Gospel meeting; but we know that they will continue to read this magazine. Do you not think that if on one page they read a love story and on the opposite page see a title such as "What Happens After Death?" they will stop to find out? Of course they will. People are interested in their souls—their need of satisfaction in this life and their fate in the world to come. But they will not reach for the bait if it is not there. Unless you and I drop the bait into the sea, they will not see it, let alone nibble at it. That is why we continue to publish these Gospel messages in most of the secular Greek-language newspapers and magazines of the world. We need to cast our nets into the wide sea of the world where the wandering fish are to be found. Unfortunately, a great deal of Christian work today consists of feeding the fish we have already caught, lest they leave us. The Lord associated with sinners in order to win them to Himself. We must follow His example. We must not only remain in the world, but we must aggressively reach out to the world—go where the fish are in order to catch them.

It takes great skill to fish. You have to know the right bait, as well as the right net or hook, for each kind of fish. All fish are not caught in the same way. All men are not won to Jesus Christ by the same methods. The fact that your way is successful for you does not give you the right to criticize others who use different methods. The sea is big enough for all, and any number of ways of fishing will be found successful. The main thing is to catch souls.

A sailor who had just returned from a whaling voyage was taken by a friend to hear an eloquent preacher. Afterward the friend said, "Jack, wasn't that a fine sermon?" "Yes, it was ship-shape," replied Jack; "the masts just high enough, the sails and the rigging all right; but I did not see any harpoons. When a vessel goes on a whaling voyage, the great thing is to get whales, but they do not come because you have a fine ship; you must go after them and harpoon them. The preacher must be the whaler." But let us remember that not all of us can catch whales. Some of us can only catch sardines. That's perfectly all right as long as we catch something.

During the first and second centuries, the sign of Christianity was the fish. A present-day Christian decided that a fishhook would be the proper emblem for a soul-winner to use for winning people to Christ, so he had a little golden fishhook made to be worn on the lapel of his coat, and when people asked him what it meant he told them that he was a fisher of men. A little newsboy from whom he bought a paper one day said to him, "Mister, do you belong to a fishing club?" "Yes, I do," said the Christian, "and I think fishing is pretty nice, don't you?" "Oh yes," the little fellow replied. "Do you ever catch any big ones?" "I have caught 250-pounders," replied the man. "Go on!" said the lad incredulously. "Yes," said the Christian. "I have caught a 250-pound fish." "Those sure are big," marveled the boy. Then leaning over, the Christian said, "Sonny, to tell you the truth, I'd rather catch small fish than big ones." He exclaimed. "No!" "Yes, about your size." The little boy looked down at himself as if he were thinking, "I'm not so small." Then the Christian told him that he was a fisher of men, seeking to win souls, and that if he would believe on the Lord Jesus Christ he would be saved. The newsboy took him at his word and came to Christ. Here was a fisherman for Christ who used a gold fishhook on his lapel to catch souls with. You may have some other kind of hook. It makes no difference, as long as you catch fish.

It is deeply satisfying to belong to the greatest fishing club in the world—composed of Christians who become fishers of men and seek out men, women, and children everywhere to lead them to Christ.